SO YOU HAVE TO GIVE A SPEECH!

MARGARET RYAN

SO YOU HAVE TO GIVE A SPEECH!

FRANKLIN WATTS I 1987
NEW YORK I LONDON I TORONTO I SYDNEY
A LANGUAGE POWER BOOK

Photographs courtesy of:
© 1981 Steve Friedman: pp. 15, 16, 19,
40, 87, 107, 111, 117, 118, 119;
UPI/Bettmann Newsphotos: pp. 18, 38;
Rothco Cartoons: pp. 22, 72, 73, 79;
AP/Wide World: pp. 29, 31, 54, 93, 99.

Library of Congress Cataloging-in-Publication Data

Ryan, Margaret.
So you have to give a speech!

(A Language power book)
Bibliography : p.
Includes index.
Summary: A guide to writing and delivering a speech,
from choosing a topic, through research and doing a
draft, to actual delivery.
1. Public speaking—Juvenile literature. [1. Public
speaking] I. Title II. Series.
PN4121.P915   1987   808.5'1   86-23354
ISBN 0-531-10337-4

FOR EMILY

CONTENTS

ALSO BY
MARGARET RYAN

Filling Out a Life
(poetry)

SO YOU HAVE TO
GIVE A SPEECH!

SO YOU HAVE TO GIVE A SPEECH

1

Most people would rather die than give a speech. In fact, when a recent survey revealed what Americans fear most, death was fourth on the list; giving a speech was first.

Even veteran speechmakers suffer from fear of public speaking. One vice-president of a $12 million corporation visibly trembles on his way to the podium each time he has to address a group—about once a week. And anyone who has coached speakers can tell you there are only two kinds: those who let their fear stop them, and those who take their fear with them, who put it to work.

Speechmaking is probably no mystery to you. Maybe you haven't been asked to give one before, but we've all seen and heard plenty of speeches: politicians on television, the principal over the PA, parents at town meetings, our classmates at assembly or commencement. One important fact about speeches is immediately obvious: some are more interesting than others.

What are you afraid of? Your audience will automatically be impressed by the fact that you're the one brave enough to give the speech!

What makes the words of one speaker catch our imagination and linger in our memories, while others are forgotten before we're even out the door? Talent may separate the truly great from the competent, but talent alone does not make a great speech. *Preparation makes performance possible.* Good speakers know and practice the steps that lead to an interesting, effective speech.

As members of the audience, of course, we don't usually see the preparation—only its results. In this respect, speeches are like athletic events. We applaud and admire the polished routine of a gymnast, but unless we are athletes or trainers or students of the sport ourselves, the rigorous training, the repetition and practice that make the routine flawless, remain invisible. The difference between a gold medalist and an also-ran includes talent, but all the talent in the world won't make up for preparation, persistence, and practice.

If you have any fear of giving a speech, and "I've never done it before" is part of the reason, take heart. Giving a speech is a skill, like driving a car, knitting a sweater, or playing a video game. It can be learned.

You already know a great deal that will help you give a speech, beginning with your knowledge of yourself, for your speaking style will be an outgrowth of your personality. If you are the witty, outgoing type, you will probably be most successful as a humorous, exuberant speaker. If you tend to be more retiring, perhaps more at home with books or computers or pets than you are onstage, your style may be reserved and thoughtful.

Whatever your style, it should always be an expression of who you are. There is room on the podium for the speaker of meticulous preparation and careful expression, for the emotional speaker whose stories of courage or compassion can move crowds to tears or to action, as well as for the witty speaker who makes us laugh. In fact, the most successful speakers are those who combine good humor, clear thinking, and emotional appeal—and who are comfortable being themselves in front of an audience.

You will find, as you prepare and give a speech, that some aspects of the process will come easily to you. You might be great at thinking up topics, at researching, or at delivering your address. Appreciate your strengths and build on them. Other parts of the process may be more difficult for you: perhaps organizing your thoughts, or modulating your voice, or thinking up attention-getting openings will be your challenge. With practice, these parts of speechmaking will get easier.

Learning to give a speech will help you fulfill the assignment that led you to this book in the first place. It will also provide you with a skill that remains useful. You will find speaking ability important to your academic career, and to your professional development once school is behind you. One manager I know had been branded a technician, and had been limited in her opportunities to advance, until she was asked to fill in for her boss and make a speech. Once top management realized she not only had good ideas, but could also express them persuasively in front of an audience, the long-awaited promotion came her way.

There are other less tangible rewards for acquiring speaking skills: the excitement of having an audience really listening, and thinking about what you have to say; the satisfaction of expressing your thoughts clearly and persuasively. There is even some pleasure to be derived from giving a speech: the vice-president who trembles on the way to the podium also cherishes the exhilaration he experiences once the speech is done.

Even if you're one of the lucky few who have no fear of speaking, you'll find that learning how to prepare will

Speeches are given in many situations
and settings, by presidents addressing
the nation to individuals addressing
other people while sitting around a
table. Speeches of one kind or another
are part of the fabric of our lives.

make your job easier. This book outlines a step-by-step process used by business and profesional speakers, by speakers who entertain, as well as by those who persuade and instruct. It can lead you toward a confident performance behind the podium.

But the book can take you just so far. Only you can put this system for successful speaking into action; only you can prepare, practice, and perfect your own successful speaking style.

WHAT SHOULD
I TALK ABOUT?

2

*In Maine we have a saying
that there's no point
in speaking unless you can
improve on silence.*

Edmund Muskie

In order to improve on silence, you will need a solid topic for your speech. And not just any topic: one about which *you* have something to say. A good speech entertains, instructs, informs, amuses, perhaps even amazes or impresses; it wins votes, hearts, a good grade, or an oratory contest. What you say may be orig-inal, it may be witty, it may be wise. But no matter what approach you take, your topic must be something that interests you.

This is your chance to have your say, so take time to find and focus in on a topic that fits your tastes, one that you have some feeling for. That feeling may be positive

"What this country really *needs* is a ten-cent
candy bar you can't swallow in one bite!"
[Are you sure you picked the right topic?]

or negative—you may love your topic or hate it—but if you are neutral your job will be hard. You can't expect your audience to care about what you are saying to them unless you care first. Boredom is highly contagious, and audiences have little resistance to it.

Unfortunately, speakers aren't always permitted to select their own topics. Whether you are limited by an assignment ("Give a speech on the history of Poland") or told to talk about anything—but for no more than five minutes—you will be working with a certain amount of limitation and a certain amount of choice.

Perhaps you are one of the lucky ones who know exactly what their topic is and what they want to say about it. Good for you! Go on to the next chapter and start your research. But if you find yourself having trouble choosing a subject, or struggling to bring an assigned topic down to a size and shape that you find both manageable and compelling, read on.

Let's consider all the ways topics come to you, and how you can work within each set of limitations to find a subject that speaks to you—and one you feel confident you can speak about.

- You may be assigned a subject, or given a list of suggested topics and asked to choose.
- Or you may be speaking at an occasion, such as graduation or a testimonial dinner, which will provide its own subject matter: a look toward the future, the good nature of the person being honored.
- Sometimes you will be expected to speak with a specific purpose—to entertain, to inform, or to persuade—while the subject of your talk will be left to you.
- Finally, you may be given a time limit, say, fifteen minutes, and allowed to speak on anything you like.

We'll consider each circumstance in turn.

ASSIGNED TOPICS

Whether it's one unavoidable assignment, such as the nuclear freeze, or a list of several topics from which you can choose, all assigned topics share a common flaw: they are too broad. Teachers usually assign broad topics by design; they want you to have room within an assignment to find an angle that interests you. And people who ask you to speak, while they may indicate a broad area they know will be of interest to their audience or one that will fit in with other topics on the program, will rarely dictate the precise subject for your speech.

The most important thing to do with an assigned topic is to narrow it down to size.

Let's take an example. Suppose you have been asked to make a speech about baseball and given a time limit of fifteen minutes. Obviously, you cannot cover the entire subject in that little time. So you will have to whittle down the big topic to more sensible proportions.

Begin by considering your interests. You will need an angle that appeals to you. Do you care about the history of the designated hitter? Or about the ways television has changed the game? Are you a woman who loves baseball or a man who hates it, and have you strong reasons either way? Do you think women should be allowed to play in the major leagues? Or are you more concerned with the impact Jackie Robinson made on the sport?

Perhaps you're the business type and want to know who owns the clubs, how they're financed, and the ways in which corporate ownership affects the sport. Or you're a fan concerned about the high price of tickets. Or you played Little League, and you'd like to tell others what it meant to you, and how it's shaped your appreciation of the game. Maybe you've been following the drug testing conflict in the major leagues. Or you're wondering if Japanese baseball is different from, and similar to, the game you grew up watching.

You can see that even within a topic such as baseball, you can find an almost infinite number of fifteen-minute topics. Is one better than another? Yes. How do you know which one it is? It is the one that most interests you.

But what if you have trouble thinking up topics to choose from? One way to crack your subject is to ask yourself the kinds of questions reporters ask: who, what, when, where, why, and how.

- Who in baseball interests you?
- What made baseball the national pastime?
- Why does anyone care about baseball?
- When did baseball begin? How has it changed over time?
- Who has changed it? What are the forces affecting it now?
- Where is baseball played, and who's playing it?
- How is baseball different from or similar to other sports, other national pastimes?

The answers to these questions should generate information that will lead you to a topic you can care about.

And, in addition to the five w's and how, don't forget to ask yourself, "How do I feel about it?" If you think the whole idea of grown men dressing in uniforms and running around bases is ridiculous, you may have found the angle you need to turn a broad topic into a manageable one.

BRAINSTORMING

Try brainstorming if your topic doesn't generate any immediately exciting notions. It's easy and fun to do. Write your topic in the center of a sheet of paper, and then scribble around it all the ideas you can think of.

Don't be too hard on your ideas. Just let yourself go—think them up and write them down. Let yourself be ridiculous and outrageous. Sometimes wild ideas make the best speeches.

If you find yourself staring at the topic and unable to come up with a single thought, try brainstorming with a friend. Again, just write down all the ideas you have.

When you've emptied your head of ideas and set them all down on paper, take a few minutes to read them over and think them through. Try to figure out why you thought of Cadillacs when the subject was baseball. Is the connection interesting? Does it lead you toward a workable topic?

When you've thought about all the possible angles, select the three strongest ideas, and consider them in more depth. Which one do you like best? Which would be easiest to research, in terms of both the time and the resources available to you? Which would be hardest to talk about, and why? Which would be the most fun for you? For your audience?

Next, take your time limit into account. Most speeches allow you to present only a single strong idea, along with supporting reasons, arguments, and information. For example, you probably won't be able to discuss both baseball in Japan and women in the major leagues in a single speech, unless you are talking about women in major league Japanese baseball.

And one main idea is all your audience will absorb, no matter how much you try to fit in. The "less is more" theory holds especially true in speechmaking: you can make one point superbly, two well, three weakly, and so on. Try to keep your topic straightforward and simple. Remember that a speech is not a dissertation.

Once you've got your topic, you need to be sure you've got an angle on it, a point of view. What is the main thing you want to say about women in baseball? Or about Little League? Consider these topics and angles:

Topic	Angle
Women in baseball	Women should be allowed to play in the major leagues
	Keep women out of baseball!
Japanese baseball	More American than our own
	Another game
Corporate ownership	New life for an old sport
	The death of the spirit of baseball

Any of the angles listed would make good, manageable fifteen-minute speech material. How do you choose? Again, the best criterion is what interests you, how you feel about the subject.

What if none of the ideas you came up with grabs you strongly? Try to give yourself a little time. You may find one topic keeps floating up into consciousness, nagging at you when you least expect it. If so, that's the one. If none of them grabs you, go back and brainstorm a little more if you have time.

If you don't have time—and let's face it, sometimes you won't—close your eyes, pick a topic, and go with it. The more strongly you feel about what you are going to say, the better your speech will be, but sometimes just doing the assignment is all you can handle. Don't worry about it. You may find yourself caring more as you learn more about your subject. Or your research may lead you to tweak your topic a little, to put a spin on it that makes it more intriguing. Just pick the topic you feel warmest toward, and go for it.

SPEAKING TO AN OCCASION

Whether it's a graduation ceremony, a preelection rally, a testimonial dinner, or an award ceremony, certain speaking occasions come with their own ready-made subject matter. While this at first seems to solve your problems, it does create some others: your job is to find a fresh angle on a well-worn subject, an angle that not only make it interesting for your audience, but one that also makes it your own.

Professional speechwriters are often asked to write "occasional" speeches. Their solution to the problem of "making it new" is to take advantage of every detail of an event. Make use of the specifics that make this graduation, or testimonial, or rally different from every one that's ever taken place.

For example, when the American Adventure pavilion at Walt Disney's Epcot Center was being dedicated, the speechwriter's challenge was to say, "We are glad to be sponsoring this building," in a way that engaged the audience. To breathe life into the topic, she took advantage of the date of the ceremony—Columbus Day—and began by referring to Christopher Columbus's "trip" and the assistance provided by Queen Isa-

The first draft of the most famous speech ever written for an occasion —the Gettysburg Address.

First Draft.

Executive Mansion,

Washington,   186

Four score and seven years ago our fathers brought forth, upon this continent, a new nation, conceived in liberty, and dedicated to the proposition that "all men are created equal"

Now we are engaged in a great civil war, testing whether that nation, or any nation so conceived, and so dedicated, can long endure. We are met on a great battle field of that war. We have come to dedicate a portion of it, as a final resting place for those who died here, that the nation might live. This we may, in all propriety do. But, in a larger sense, we can not dedicate— we can not consecrate— we can not hallow, this ground— The brave men, living and dead, who struggled here, have hallowed it, far above our poor power to add or detract. The world will little note, nor long remember what we say here; while it can never forget what they did here.

It is rather for us, the living, to stand here,

ted to the great task remaining before us— that, from these honored dead we take in creased devotion to that cause for which they here, gave the last full measure of de= votion— that we here highly resolve these dead shall not have died in vain; that the nation, shall have a new birth of free— dom, and that government of the people by the people for the people, shall not per= ish from the earth.

bella. Images of travel, travel services, and the discovery of America tied in neatly to American Express, with its travel services, participating in the sponsorship of a building called "the American Adventure." It was enough to turn a dull subject into a brief, fresh speech.

Take a tip from the professionals. For an occasional speech, ask yourself:

- Is the date/season/time of year related to the event in any significant way? Did anything else happen on this date which can be related to the subject of my speech? (Check an almanac: you may find yourself speaking on the day the *Titanic* sank, or the day humans first walked on the moon.)
- What would people at the first event such as this think of this one? How was the first graduating class from your high school different from this class, for example?
- How would this occasion look to people in the future—ten, twenty, or fifty years from now?
- How would this event look to a figure in history? A creature from another planet? A movie star? Someone from another country or culture?

Finding a fresh perspective is the key. But remember, whatever interesting facts you turn up must be tied

Martin Luther King addressing a huge crowd in front of the Lincoln Memorial during the March on Washington civil rights demonstration in 1963. Dr. King was an eloquent and powerful speaker.

back into the event at hand. They must be relevant to *your* audience, *your* event.

SPEECHES WITH
A PURPOSE

Suppose you've been told to give a speech with a specific purpose—to inform, say, or to persuade—and the topic of the speech is left entirely up to you.

Of course, you know that you must pick a topic that interests you; it's no good trying to inform an audience about stamp collecting if the sight of stamps makes you sick. Similarly, you can't persuade your listeners to care about the current state of the judicial system if thinking about it makes you yawn.

If you've been asked to give a speech that informs, begin by taking a look at your interests. List the three things you currently care about most. How much do you know about each? Can you speak from close or personal experience on the difficulty of breaking into the music business? Could you fill an audience in on ways to create computer graphics? Or are robots and their uses your special concern? Maybe you've been studying the English flower garden in preparation for spring planting, and you now know more about Gertrude Jekyll's color schemes than anyone else in town. Chances are you have some special interest you can share.

With informational speeches, it's best to work from what you know, rather than things you'd like to know about. This is no time to unravel the intricacies of unified field theory. Unless you already have a solid grounding in astrophysics, you probably won't have time to get the facts down yourself, let alone develop a perspective that would make for an interesting speech.

And don't worry if the things you know about—baseball, robots, how to give a perfect manicure or groom a horse—don't sound as impressive as the time-space continuum. Your audience will probably prefer learning something useful that you really know about to being lectured on concepts even you have trouble handling.

If you've been asked to persuade, you'll need to take a position you believe in—or at least, one that you feel is defensible. Though it is sometimes interesting to play devil's advocate and create reasons to support something you don't agree with, as a sort of intellectual exercise, it's probably more fun for you than for your audience. Save the devil's advocate role for some other occasion, and choose a topic you care about.

When you've got your subject, ask yourself what you would like to have your audience believe or do when your speech is finished—that is, what do you want to persuade them to do? By talking about subjects that touch the lives of your audience closely, by persuading them about situations in which they can have an impact, you create a better opportunity for yourself to give a gripping speech.

To argue that America should stop spending more than it has, or that the countries of the world should ban the bomb, may be interesting and easy to justify, but what do you want your audience to do? Tackle an issue closer to home: persuade your audience how important it is to develop a lifelong interest in sports, or to eat right, or to preserve their First Amendment rights in the school newspaper.

Remember that in persuasive speeches, you can appeal to reason or to the emotions or better yet, you can appeal to both. But in any case, you need a topic both you and your audience can feel connected to and care about.

YOUR CHOICE

Having total freedom to choose a topic is either the best or worst situation to be in. It's clearly the best if you're very sure about what you want to say. It can be the worst if you feel you have so much to say, about so many things, that you can't quite bring yourself to focus. It can also be the worst if you feel you just have nothing to say.

As with narrowing down assigned topics, there are a few basic rules that might help.

- Choose a topic that interests you.
- Choose a topic you know something about.
- Choose a topic that you have strong feelings about.
- Choose a topic that suits your time limits.Decide whether your purpose is to inform or to persuade . . . or to entertain.
- Pick a topic you can research and write about in the time available to you.
- Develop an angle that you can speak from. Nurture a point of view.
- Pick a topic that will appeal to your audience.

No matter how you've arrived at your topic, it's time now to state your subject in a way that you can work with. It will no longer be baseball; it might be "Why Women Should Play in the Major Leagues." It should not be "Graduation," though it might be "Education: A Life's Work." State your topic clearly, briefly, strongly. And remember to state it in such a way that it expresses your feelings, thoughts, or opinions about the subject, and in a way that will appeal to your audience.

In fact, no matter how you have arrived at your topic—by hard work, or by having it handed to you—you will have to think about your audience and how they will respond to it. Who they are, what they know and don't know about your subject, and what brought them to your speech in the first place will all influence both the research you do and the way that your speech takes shape.

ASSESSING YOUR AUDIENCE

3

*The best audience is
one that is intelligent,
well educated—and
a little drunk.*

Alben W. Barkley

Witticisms aside, the best audience is one you have taken the time to get acquainted with, at least imaginatively, before standing up at the podium. Who you are speaking to, what they know, how they feel about your subject, what they have been doing before and what they will be doing after your speech—these are all factors that will color, however subtly, your presentation of your topic.

Try to think of your speech as a product, one you will be marketing to your audience. Companies don't just dream up ideas, spend millions to produce them, and introduce the results to the public. First, they do intensive market research, to make sure that what they make will fill buyers' needs.

Millions of dollars are spent every year on surveys, and more millions on test marketing, to discover what people want, how much they want it, how much they are willing to pay for it, and how often they would buy it. These facts are collected, analyzed, studied, reported on, and researched again long before the first product makes it to the production line.

Of course, you will not need to do extensive market research before writing your speech. You can't sit down with your audience beforehand to ask what they think about your topic or what they'll be having for lunch the day of your talk. But you can give some thought to who these listeners will be, what mood they will be in, and the conditions under which they will be listening to you. You can tailor your speech so that it has the best chance of being "bought," that is, avidly listened to by your audience.

When thinking about your audience, begin with the reporter's five questions: who, what, when, where, and why.

Whom will you be speaking to? Be specific. Adults, teenagers, or children? Or a mixture of all three? You will use different language when addressing the third grade on voting than when addressing the League of Women Voters.

Will the audience be all men, all women, or a mixture? And, if a mixture, what proportion of each? While you will never make a sexist remark—a comment that could insult men or women by its very nature—you may want to vary the statistics, examples, or anecdotes you include in your speech based on the male/female ratio.

Is it a large or a small group? Small groups tend to be more intimate, to pay closer attention, and they tend to share opinions. Large groups are by their nature

more diverse, and you may need more compelling examples, language, imagery, and style to keep their attention.

What do they already know and believe about your subject? Are you speaking about stamp collecting to your speech class, or to a group of avid philatelists? Do you need to establish that baseball is a sport, or can you get right to the fine points of pitching? Are they inclined to agree with you, or are they definitely on the other side of the fence?

Your audience's level of interest—the amount of information they already have about your subject, as well as their assumptions and prejudices—will shape the structure of your speech and determine the level of detail you will need to include.

When will you be speaking? After dinner, when everyone is a little sleepy? Or first thing in the morning, when most minds are at their most alert? After-dinner speeches need to be a little lighter, more entertaining, than early-morning presentations. The morning audience is better equipped to absorb intricate and detailed information.

Think, too, about the time of year. Your speech class will have a different atmosphere on the first day of school than it will an hour before spring break starts.

Where will you be speaking? Will you be in a classroom, on stage in an auditorium, in a television studio, in a restaurant, or outdoors at a graduation? Think

Former Congresswoman Barbara Jordan of Texas, an outstanding speaker. When you have something to say that people want to hear, and you're good at saying it, people want to listen.

about how the audience will feel. Will they be comfortable or ill at ease? Consider contingencies such as weather, restaurant noise, and other events that may be going on around you.

Why have they come? Because they want to, or because they have to? Will they be eager to hear your speech, or are they captives, who will need to be entertained and enticed into listening? What does your audience hope to gain from your talk: information, an impassioned opinion, or half an hour's entertainment? Try to give them something of what they came for.

After the five w's, ask yourself one more reporter's question: how? *How would you feel in their place?* Empathize with your audience. Write the speech you would want to hear if you were sitting out there with them.

Now that you've considered your audience, and what they want, consider what effect you want to have on them. Do you want to meet their expectations, or surprise them? Satisfy the curiosity they have, or generate more questions in their minds about your subject? Do you want to get them thinking, or give them answers? Motivate them to take action, or talk them out of doing something they seem hell-bent on anyway?

Knowing both what you want to accomplish and what your audience wants and needs to hear will give you considerable guidance in the next step of preparing to speak: doing your research.

New York City Mayor Ed Koch
has the ability to rise to the
occasion in most any setting.

RESEARCH

4

Knowledge is of two kinds:
We know a subject ourselves,
or we know where we can
find information upon it.

Samuel Johnson

If you have picked a topic you are interested in, narrowed an assigned topic down to size, or thought about the requirements of the occasion you must address, and given some thought to your audience, you are ready to begin researching your speech.

Obviously, you already know something about your topic. Before you can learn more, you must take inventory of the facts, opinions, and feelings you have on hand. Taking stock of what you already know will give you a good idea of what you still need to know, and how to find it.

Putting your ideas on paper will also help you get a clear picture of what they are. Sometimes you don't even know what you're thinking about a subject until you start to put it into words. Other times, what seemed like a good idea in your head turns out to be fuzzy and unclear once it appears on paper.

Writing your ideas down will also help you see how your thoughts on the subject you've chosen relate to one another, where you need facts to support your opinions, what points you can already support with facts, and the places in which you still need to do some work.

This writing down of your ideas is not the same as writing a draft. Remember, you are taking inventory to determine what you already have and how the pieces fit. It's like opening your closet to examine your wardrobe. You are going to see what you own, what fits, what doesn't, and how the various pieces coordinate.

GETTING STARTED

Begin by writing down everything you know about your subject. You might find it helpful to write your ideas on note cards. I use [4-by-6-inch] cards, because they are small enough to carry around and big enough to really write on. Write on one side of the card only. When you are hunting for a fact you remember writing down but can't seem to find, you will be assured that it is not on the back of any of your cards, a knowledge that can save a great deal of fruitless searching.

Use one card for each new idea. Try to state each thought you have about your subject as fully as possible. Add supporting evidence, however sketchy, under the idea, like this:

Baseball players are resisting drug testing, and so should high school students.

Unions dislike drug testing because . . .

Individual players are objecting that . . .

You may not know why the unions and the players are resisting, although you know they are and that they have reasons. These are clues to the facts you will need to find. If you find an idea taking up more than a single card, be sure to number the cards as you fill them. It will make it easier to deal with the facts you have gathered later on.

When you have written out everything you already think, know, and feel about your topic, take some time to read over your ideas. Sort through them slowly, making additional notes if any come to mind. Underline the ideas which seem strongest, clearest, most useful: the words that have some power for you. These are the seeds from which your speech will grow. Copy them over onto fresh cards, writing strong simple sentences and stating your ideas as clearly as possible.

In the process of copying your key ideas, you may find that some of your statements contradict each other. Don't worry about it. You'll sort these things out later, after you've done your research. For now, formulate assertions: Students' First Amendment rights are threatened by the school board's censorship of the high school paper. Perennials are the backbone of the English floral border. Robots improve both our technological processes and the products they manufacture.

If opposing opinions come to mind as you create your assertions, so much the better. Write them down, too. Answering objections is important in certain types of speeches, and you can't answer them if you don't know what they are: Student publications aren't covered by the First Amendment of the U.S. Constitution. Although colorful, perennials bloom only for a short time. Robots are taking jobs away from human workers.

By now, you should have some idea of the kinds of information you need to find. Use your index cards to make a list of the information you're after. Is it a book about robots, or statistics on unemployment and its causes? Are you trying to find an article on baseball players you saw a few weeks ago, in either *Time* or *Sports Illustrated*, but you're not sure which? Do you think you'd like a quote from some famous English gardener to support some of your own observations?

Put down, as specifically as you can, what you need to know. Don't worry if your list isn't complete or entirely clear: part of the fun of research is stumbling across unexpected, interesting, useful information while you're hot on the trail of something else entirely.

Whether you need quotes from major league players, union leader's pronouncements on the use of robots in Detroit, the text of the First Amendment, or a list of perennial plants, your next stop should be the library.

USING THE LIBRARY

The best source of information in the library is not a book, a magazine, an index, an abstract, or a piece of microfilm. It is a human being, the librarian. Try talking to your librarian before you dive into the card catalog or the *Reader's Guide to Periodical Literature.* Chances are, your librarian will be pleased to help and will speed your search for information.

Begin by introducing yourself. "Hi, I'm _____. I'm a student at _____, and I have to make a speech on _____. I need to find _____." Show the libararian your list, and you will soon find yourself delving into some of the following sources of information. If your librarian can't help you, you can always search out these sources for yourself.

Encyclopedias
Encyclopedias provide the big picture on a variety of topics, and can help you get a quick overview of the

subject you have chosen. General encyclopedias include *Americana, Britannica,* and *Colliers.* These are written for the common reader, so they are easy to read and may contain facts you can use.

More specialized encyclopedias, such as *The Encyclopedia of Textiles* or *The Encyclopaedic Dictionary of Physics* are better bets for specialized information. The information may be a bit more difficult for the general reader to understand, but it will be complete, detailed, and specific. Encyclopedias exist on almost every topic you can imagine. They are useful books to know about.

Yearbooks
In addition to their standard A-to-Z volumes, many encyclopedias issue annual yearbooks, which supplement and update the basic volumes. These are especially helpful if you are concerned with recent developments in a particular field.

The *Statistical Abstract of the United States* is another useful yearbook. Published by the U.S. Bureau of the Census, it contains a wealth of facts, tables, graphs, and statistics on subjects including population, education, science, energy, and many, many more. A similar book, published by the United Nations and called the *Statistical Yearbook*, offers similar information on more than 150 countries around the world.

Almanacs
Almanacs contain lists, charts, and various types of other factual information, usually from a variety of fields. The best known is *The World Almanac and Book of Facts.* It is beautifully indexed and contains an incredible assortment of information. Check it out.

Indexes
Indexes are your door into the vast array of periodical literature, that is, the magazines and newspapers that,

day after day, month after month, and year after year, supply the general reader with current information on a broad range of subjects.

The Readers' Guide to Periodical Literature lists information on articles in more than one hundred American commercial periodicals that address a general audience. Articles are indexed both by subject and by author. Entries will tell you all you need to find the article you're looking for: title of the article, the author's name, the magazine the article appeared in, the date, the volume number of the magazine—even the page number.

The New York Times Index will help you find any information that has been published in *The New York Times* during the last one hundred plus years. Major news stories are summarized in the *Index,* so even if your library can't put a set of *New York Times* microfilms at your disposal, the *Index* itself can be very useful.

Sources for Quotations

Every good library will carry several source books of quotations. The most widely available and perhaps most widely quoted source is Bartlett's *Familiar Quotations.* While this is the standard reference, I find many of the quotations are overused, overly literary, or overly long for inclusion in speeches.

Several more contemporary collections of quotations might prove to be more useful to you.

Peter's Quotations: Ideas for Our Time, edited by Dr. Laurence J. Peter, is full of varied and witty sayings. You can find quotes from Woody Allen, Joe Namath, and Albert Einstein, on topics ranging from Ability to Zoos.

Another useful source is the *Barnes & Noble Book of Quotations,* edited by Robert I. Fitzhenry. Here you'll find Gilda Radner quoted on the same page with Voltaire, and the subjects run from Ability and Achievement to Youth. This collection includes many national proverbs, which can be fun to use, such as the Irish saying "Better quarrelling than lonesome," or the Dutch "A handful of patience is worth more than a bushel of brains."

I also like to browse in *The Great Thoughts,* compiled by George Seldes, when I'm looking for a quotation or an idea. Unfortunately for speechwriters, however, it is arranged by author, from Abelard to Zola, and is not indexed by subject, so finding something that speaks to your topic often becomes a matter of pure luck.

Then there's *The Morrow Book of Quotations in American History,* by Joseph R. Conlin. It contains quotations about American life, from the Pilgrims to the present. Indexed by subject and by person quoted, this book is a wonderful source. You'll find gangsters, politicans, soldiers, statesmen, writers, artists, entertainers, and philosophers quoted on a wide range of subjects.

Still another quotation source book is *Money Talks—The 3,000 Greatest Quotes on Business from Aristotle to DeLorean.* It is edited by Robert W. Kent and is organized around the curriculum of the Harvard MBA program. The quotations in each chapter are arranged chronologically and feature a managerial or business point of view.

Books
For current topics, such as the drug testing controversy, rock music, or the growth of video technology, books tend to be less useful then periodicals. It just takes longer to get a good book into print than it does to publish a magazine article, and much of the information you find in books on really hot topics may be less than fresh.

But if you're looking for background on a current problem in politics or history or want to read up on the history of gardening, computers, robots, or space exploration, you may wish to read a book or two to give yourself a sense of the context in which current events are happening.

Use the card catalog to find books on the subject you're interested in. The card catalog is usually arranged both by subject and by author's last name, in alphabetical order. If you need help with the card catalog, ask your librarian.

Videotapes

Many libraries now stock videocassette tapes, and if your topic is business related or deals with the entertainment industry, videotapes may be just the source you're after. Many business subjects have been addressed in training tapes—everything from "how to dress for success" to "how to close a sale." If your topic is covered in a tape, try to find time to take a look at one.

AFTER YOU'VE FOUND YOUR SOURCES

Now that you've located the books, magazines, or videotapes you need, read through or view your material and make notes on the facts that will help you write a convincing speech.

Use your index cards, one for each source. At the top of the card, list the name of the book or magazine, the date of issue, the page number you're working from, and any other reference material you would need (such as library call numbers) to locate that piece of information again. Write all this information down before you make a single note.

You may be tempted to skip this step; *don't*. It is amazing how many times I have been required to go back and check my sources, and before I became rigorous about noting bibliographical information, tracking down a once-found fact a second time often proved futile.

When you've identified your source on the card, jot down the facts, quotes, anecdotes or examples you find useful. You may wish to write the facts in your own words, or you may want to copy the language exactly as it's written, so that you can quote it word for word.

RESTATING YOUR TOPIC

When you've completed your research, you may discover that your topic, or the angle you decided to take on your topic, looks different to you. You may have uncovered information which makes you think and feel differently about your subject. You may have discovered that no information is available on exactly what you wanted to speak about, but a slightly different topic has been suggested by the material you did find.

Now is the time to restate your topic, to put it in its final form, based on what your research has taught you. Try not to go after a new topic entirely, but to alter your statement of theme only as much as necessary. "Why Women Should Be Playing Major League Baseball," might become "Why Women Have Been Shut Out of Major League Sports." "Why Drug Testing Should Not Be Mandatory in Our School District" might become, as a result of your findings, "Drug Testing for Teenagers: Pro and Con."

Make whatever changes you need in your topic statement, so that you can write a speech you believe in and that your audience can believe, one based on research and evidence.

Now write your topic sentence at the top of a clean sheet of paper. Shuffle through your idea and note cards and group your supporting ideas together. Begin to build an outline by writing down the major points that support your topic statement. Leave room to fill in the details—examples, facts, quotes—that bolster each of your stated opinions. And don't forget to state objections and answer them.

Now you have an outline and are ready to write a draft.

PREPARING A DRAFT

5

Writing is the hardest way of earning a living, with the possible exception of wrestling alligators.

Olin Miller

Whether you plan to read your speech, speak from note cards, or deliver your thoughts from memory, you will benefit from writing your speech down. Yes, it's hard work to write. But it will be worth it, because you will find that many of your ideas will not crystallize unless they are forced onto paper, into words. Once your ideas are on the page, you can and will be able to take a good hard look at them, study them, push them around until they say exactly what you mean.

And it is easier to speak, even if you work from notes or from memory, if you have already mapped out the entire text of your speech. You will remember connections better. You will have an intuitive sense of how your argument builds, from having worked it through on paper.

Besides, you've done a great deal of the tough work already. If you've written down everything you know about the topic—if you've done your research—and if you've sifted through your notes to prepare a concise statement of your topic and a loose outline, you're prepared to write.

GETTING STARTED

What's that, you say? The sight of a blank sheet of paper scares you? You're blocked, you're blank, you can't think of how to begin, or once you begin, you can't think of what to say next? Welcome to the writer's world.

You should know that even experienced writers suffer something akin to terror when faced with a blank page. It is scary to write. Part of the fear comes from facing the unknown: after all, you really don't know what you are going to say until you say it. Another part of the anxiety comes from feeling that whatever you put down won't be good enough—and not necessarily for other people, but good enough for the critical side of you.

Many writers talk about the writing process as if they were in fact two people: a writer and an editor. Whatever words the writer puts on the page, the editor will manage to find fault with them. "That's silly!" the editor says. "You can't start with 'I'! You don't know what you're doing. What makes you think you can write a good speech?"

If these sound like voices you've heard in your head when you sit down to write, take heart. Your editor, the critical part of you that keeps you from writing, is a

handy sort to have around—once the actual writing is done and the editing has started. You will need that critical awareness to help you find and remove excess language, insert commas, correct spelling, and generally determine whether you are communicating effectively through the words you've chosen.

However, having that editor on hand during the process of setting words down on paper can lead to writer's block. So tell that critical part of you to take a hike, to take a nap, to take a vacation until after you've written your first draft. Until that draft exists in its entirety, you are only a writer, involved only in putting your ideas into words and setting those words on a page.

If your critic is persistent and nagging, as mine is, you may have to resort to some time-honored tricks to shake the editor loose long enough for you to write. Here are some that have worked for professional writers, and just may work for you.

WRITING BEFORE THE CRITIC IS AWAKE

Get up an hour earlier than usual in the morning and go directly to your desk or other work area. Write everything you know about your speech without stopping. Get out as much as you can. If this works, but you don't get it all down in one day, try it again on successive mornings.

New York Governor Mario Cuomo has moved ahead politically in great part because of his speech-making prowess. He reportedly writes all his own speeches and spends a great deal of time and effort choosing his words.

Be careful not to read or listen to the radio or watch television before you begin. You don't want the critic to wake up before you get as many words on the page as possible. Don't worry about whether the words are the perfect ones or if you're writing everything in exactly the order you should. Follow your outline loosely, letting yourself stray as much as you want to, pulling yourself gently back to the subject at hand if you think you have wandered too far afield.

TIRING THE CRITIC OUT

If for some reason you can't get up before your critic is awake, you can always try tiring your critic out.

First, make sure your work area is ready for you. Set out paper and pens or pencils, your typewriter—whatever tools you need to write. Look over your outline, reading it to yourself several times. Then set it down, and leave the house.

Indulge in some solitary sport for at least at hour. Take a very long walk, or jog, or swim—whatever appeals to you. Try to keep your topic gently in mind as your exercise, but don't force yourself to think of it. During the last part of the hour and as you head back to your desk or other workplace, picture yourself sitting down and effortlessly writing everything you know about your topic.

When you reach your prepared workplace, sit down and begin to write immediately. Say everything you know about your speech on paper. Again, don't worry if what you write sounds silly or confused. You'll straighten it out during the revision process. Drafts can always be improved, as long as they exist. Getting something down, no matter how small a corner of your ideas, gives you a way into the rest of them. Just write.

If you have no quiet place to work at home, plan to end up at a library. Carry your notebook or pad and pens and pencils with you. When you arrive, find a spot, sit down, and begin to write immediately.

THE PROBLEM
OF PROCRASTINATION

Maybe you have no problem writing once you get started, but starting itself is a problem. Perhaps you're always putting off writing until the last minute, telling yourself you work better under pressure and leaving barely enough time to write a first draft, let alone revise and polish it.

If that pattern sounds familiar, you are suffering from procrastination. It can be cured. The simplest way to get around it is to work with a kitchen timer. Set the timer for twenty minutes and promise yourself you will write without stopping until the bell rings.

It doesn't matter if you spend the first ten minutes writing nonsense; that often happens. If you keep putting one word after another on the paper, writing without a pause, you will eventually come around to your subject. Once you've begun, it will be easier to go on. Remember, don't stop until the bell rings.

When your twenty minutes are over, stop writing and reward yourself. Take a walk, have a snack, watch part of a favorite TV show, or listen to some music—whatever gives you pleasure. Then set the timer again for another twenty minutes, and again, write. Do as many twenty-minute sessions as it takes you to get a complete first draft on the page.

Sometimes we procrastinate because the job at hand seems overwhelming. If that's your problem, try breaking it down into small segments. Write the opening in one session, write the close another time, then fill in the middle.

Whatever method you choose, work regularly; then reward yourself for accomplishment.

THINK POSITIVE

If lack of confidence keeps you from writing, try giving yourself positive messages instead of the negative ones you're probably working from now. Tell yourself you *can* do it. Repeat to yourself, as often as possible, encouraging words such as, "I can write this speech. I know a lot about my subject."

You don't even have to believe the positive messages you send yourself. They'll work if you keep repeating them, whether you believe them or not.

NOW THAT YOU'RE READY TO WRITE

You have your outline prepared. You know your main ideas, and the order in which they should appear. You've planned, if necessary, to outsmart your critic, work through your procrastination, and build your confidence. But how do you actually put your ideas into words?

There is a simple time-tested formula for giving a speech, and here it is. It may sound boring, it may sound old-fashioned, but it never fails. Every speech has three parts:

1. A beginning
2. A middle
3. An end.

In that order. And each part of the speech serves a clear and necessary function.

The beginning: tell them what you are going to tell them.
The middle: tell them.
The end: tell them what you have told them.

That's it. If it sounds easy, it is. Here's how it works in more detail.

TELL THEM WHAT YOU'RE GOING TO TELL THEM: PREPARING PEOPLE TO HEAR WHAT YOU'RE ABOUT TO SAY

What does it mean to tell your audience what you're going to tell them? You could say, "Today I'm going to talk about baseball, and why I think women should be allowed to play in the major leagues." And if you did, it would be a clear, simple, and direct beginning.

But would it get your audience's attention? Would it arouse their interest, perk up their ears, and make them want to hear more? Probably not. And that is exactly what your opening should do: while it states your topic, it should also create an appetite in your listeners for the rest of the speech.

Because your first sentences will prepare the audience for what is to follow, much as an appetizer prepares you for the dinner that is to come, it pays to give your opening a great deal of thought. Usually, you will not be able to write a really good opening until after you have completed a draft. Or as one student put it, "How can I know how to prepare the audience for what's to come, when I don't even know what's coming yet?"

That being the case, you may want to begin your draft by saying, "Today I am going to talk about . . ." and go back and rewrite your opening later. Or you may want to consider one of these tried and true ways to begin.

Use a quote. Sometimes the best words to begin with belong to someone else. Quotes can be gripping, precise, amusing, naughty, or shocking. You can quote from one of your sources, from an expert in your field, or from a famous wit, such as Oscar Wilde or Will Rogers. If you do quote from a public figure famous for using language but not necessarily well versed in your topic, be sure to connect the saying back to your subject and your point of view. You can quote someone you agree with or someone you think is all wrong. But whomever you quote, choose carefully, always keeping in mind your audience and the effect you wish to have on them.

Sometimes the most unlikely sources of sayings can be used to make a point. One successful writer I know began a speech on international marketing by quoting a person he identified as "a very successful market analyst." "I don't even know what street Canada is on," this famous marketeer was quoted as saying. What gave the beginning its punch? The revelation that the words belonged to Al Capone.

Another speechwriter I know, who had to explain why a product announced years before was just now being introduced, quoted Gypsy Rose Lee, "Anything worth doing is worth doing slowly."

In other words, you don't have to use a quote that has to do directly with your subject. Just make sure that the quote you use can be tied to your topic—and that you provide the link.

Think, too, about the kind of people you want to quote. If you expect your audience might be a little groggy after lunch, you may want to use a quote that will shock—and then disagree with it. For instance, you might begin a speech upholding the idea of the military draft by quoting Emma Goldman, a revolutionary, who said, "All wars are wars among thieves who are too cowardly to fight and who therefore induce the young manhood of the whole world to do the fighting for them." You could then go on to differ with Goldman, and tell why it is necessary to keep a standing army, and why the draft is the best way to do it.

Don't think of books of quotations as your only source of quotable material. Listen to political speeches, read current magazines and cartoons, and listen to comedians. Proverbs also make good quotes to begin speeches with, as do tag lines from current or well-known television commercials. (Remember Walter Mondale asking Ronald Reagan, "Where's the beef?")

Ask a question. If in your speech you are setting out to answer a specific question or set of questions, you might begin by asking them. "What drove America into World War II?" "Why aren't women allowed to play major league baseball?" or "What's wrong with drug testing every American high school student?" would each make an appropriate opening for a speech.

Tell an anecdote. Anecdotes, short accounts of interesting or humorous incidents, can also be effective openings for speeches.

Where do you find good anecdotes? Usually, you have to make them up. You'll need to be something of a fiction writer, creating just the tale you need to make your point.

For instance, suppose you want to begin your speech against drug testing with an anecdote. You wish to illustrate the fact that drug tests are far from foolproof, that in fact they give false results more often than not.

So you make up a character, Melissa Jones, an honor student, editor of her school yearbook, head cheerleader. Well liked, smart, a good kid. Along with everyone else in her mythical high school, she is tested for drug use. The test shows cocaine in her system.

Her parents are understandably furious. She is thrown off the cheerleading squad, asked to resign from the yearbook. Her boyfriend drops her. Her friends' parents say they can't see her. Doesn't the test prove she's on drugs?

Well, no. Eventually, the test is shown to have given a false positive. Melissa is cleared of the suspicion of using drugs, but her life has been changed forever.

Having created an anecdote that illustrates your story and engages your audience, you can then go on to tell in less emotional terms why drug testing in your school is a bad idea.

Start with a joke. Use a joke only if it's closely tied to your subject, if it's really funny, and if you can deliver it well. Also, be careful to avoid jokes that are racist, sexist, ethnic, dirty, or ageist, that is, any joke that might offend all or part of your audience.

If you do choose to begin with a joke, remember that its purpose is not to loosen the audience up or to prove that you're a likeable person. LIke any other opening, its function is to get your audience ready to hear what you have to say.

Begin with facts. A single shocking fact, or a number of shocking statistics that build to a climax, can make your audience hungry to hear the rest of what you have to say.

For example, you might begin a speech in favor of drug testing by quoting recent national surveys indicating over 80 percent of America's high school students have experimented with cocaine, that more than 60 percent of America's work force uses recreational drugs, and that American productivity is estimated to be reduced by X percent because of drug usage by workers.

For a speech in favor of raising the drinking age to twenty-one, you could quote the shocking statistics on teenage drunk driving arrests—and deaths.

For a speech on improving American women's access to technological careers, you might start with the fact that in most industrialized countries, more than 50 percent of the engineers are women, while in the United States, women comprise only 8 percent of professional engineers.

Whatever statistics you choose, make sure they are compelling, be certain they are accurate, and present them in a way that makes the fact easy for readers to comprehend.

Round off numbers. Don't say "Of every 457,005 teenagers, X number will be killed while driving drunk." Use half a million. Your audience will hear it more easily.

Make the numbers easy to see. If you're explaining exactly how big a dinosaur is, compare it to something else large—a two-story building, St. Patrick's Cathedral—something your audience can quickly grasp.

Challenge an assumption—or two. Because you've thought about your audience, you have some sense of what they assume. So you might begin your speech by challenging and overturning those assumptions.

For example, you're speaking to the varsity baseball team, and you know they aren't wild about the idea of women in professional baseball. You know their assumptions: women aren't strong enough, can't run fast enough, and can't pitch to save their souls. You might begin by reporting on any studies that show women are stronger than men, can run as fast, and can learn to pitch. Once those assumptions are overthrown, you can go on to state why you think women should be allowed into the major leagues.

TELL THEM: THE BODY OF THE SPEECH

Now that your audience knows what you're talking about, and is ready to hear more, it's time to tell them your main points, to make assertions backed up by evidence.

There are as many ways to organize the body of a speech as there are topics. The way you select will depend on both your topic and on your audience. Consider a few of the possibilities.

Deductive and inductive approaches. Deduction and induction are two ways of presenting evidence and arriving at conclusions. You use the deductive method when you present your main idea up front and then provide the details. In inductive reasoning, you build your case by providing the details first, arriving at your main idea later in the speech.

The format you choose depends to a large extent on how you expect your audience to respond to your ideas. For example, let's suppose you are giving a speech against drug testing in your high school to members of your class, whom you suspect will also oppose it. You would use the deductive plan, stating your opposition early in the speech and then providing your reasons. Using a deductive format, you let your audience know up front that you agree with them and then provide the reasons why.

But suppose you were speaking on the same topic to the school board, which was largely in favor of such testing. In that case, you would not begin by stating your opinion. To do so might alienate your audience; they might stop listening before you got to state the reasons behind your stance.

Instead, you would give your reasons, one by one, and build to your conclusion: that for reason A, reason B, and reason C, drug testing is not a good idea and should not be adopted. By using the inductive format, you give yourself time to win your audience over a little, before you present an opinion that is different from their own.

Inductive and deductive formats are often used in speeches that attempt to persuade.

Chronology. Some speeches, of course, are not persuasive; instead, they try to inform an audience about a set of facts. Or, within a persuasive speech, you may wish to trace the history or development of an attitude, an idea, or a situation.

In these cases, you might consider organizing the body of your speech chronologically, that is, according to the time at which each event happened. Talks about the history of the designated hitter, the development of robotics, or the growth cycle of the redwood tree would all benefit from the use of chronological order.

While it's usually easy to organize information chronologically (this happened, then this, then this . . .), be aware that there are pitfalls. The biggest potential problem is dullness and predictability. Most people know that trees start from seeds, become seedlings, and grow bigger, or that the Great Depression preceded World War II, which preceded the Baby Boom.

To counteract the tendency toward predictability, use lively language and fresh examples.

You might also begin, as the epic poets did, at the climax of your story, in the middle of things. Then you can go back to the beginning and show the path of events and circumstances that led to that climax. For example, you might begin a speech on the causes of World War II with the bombing of Pearl Harbor, then backtrack to the end of World War I and the Treaty of Versailles, to show how that treaty engendered the next World War.

Cause and effect. Another way to arrange the body of your speech is in terms of cause and effect. Tell your audience what events led to the current situation. For instance, if you are discussing events which led to the development of alternative energy sources, you might wish to mention the Arab oil embargo of the early 1970s, which created a shortage of oil products and higher prices. These higher prices in turn affected the U.S. balance of payments and the growth of the U.S. economy and led to government tax incentives and credits for the development of solar, wind, and other energy sources.

Geographical order. If your subject is countries on a continent, placement of factories or air bases, the movement of people in a great migration, or any other topic based on geography, organize your material geographically.

Begin in the north and work south, or start in the east and work west. You can even begin in the center and work out, as long as you choose a starting point and announce your direction early in the speech. "I'll begin with the northern region, and work toward the south." This makes it easier for your audience to follow your words.

Quantitative order. If you are discussing the ten biggest diamond deposits on earth, you can begin with the largest and work toward the smallest, or vice versa. In general, it's best to work from the smallest to the largest, from the least to the most impressive. Think of it this way: if you start with the biggest, you can lose your audience's attention as you move down the line. If you start small and build, audience interest usually builds with you.

Transitions. No matter which way of organizing your material you choose, you will need to move smoothly and strongly from one point to the next. Think of transitions as both signposts and bridges. Transitions tell your audience where you are in your speech, and lead them forward from one idea to the next. Consider some of the following:

Let's begin on the east coast . . .
Moving now to the heartland . . .
Finally, in the far west . . .

First, think about the color of your garden . . .
Second, give some thought to the height of the plants . . .

Next, take season of bloom into account . . .
Finally, map your garden on graph paper . . .

The smallest of the three major oil deposits is located . . .
The next largest deposit is . . .
But the most impressive reservoir can be found . . .

If you find yourself writing, or saying, things such as "I'd like to talk about the second largest diamond in the world, but before I do, let me digress . . ." go back and rethink the order of your speech. Weak and wordy transitions appear when something is in the wrong place. When ideas flow logically, you won't need a great many words to get from one to another.

TELL THEM WHAT YOU TOLD THEM: WAYS TO CLOSE

It's important to remind your audience of what you've said when you reach the end of your speech. This is your chance to sum it all up, memorably, and send them off with something to think about.

Think of your speech as a circle, with the close coming around to connect again with the opening.

If you used a quotation to start, refer to it as you end.

If you began with a question, restate it and provide the answer.

If you told an anecdote, recall the characters, and tell how things turned out for them, or how they might have been different had your plan been adopted.

If you began with a joke, repeat the punchline—with a twist.

If you started off with shocking facts, tell how the action you propose could alter those statistics.

If you opened by challenging assumptions, conclude by affirming the new ideas your introduced.

OTHER WAYS TO CLOSE

Of course, there's no law that says you can't use a different closing. But whatever technique you choose, make sure your finish is strong. It will be the last thing your audience hears, the words they are most likely to recall later.

Use a quote to introduce your final paragraph, or to conclude it. Choose one that summarizes your ideas, that sounds conclusive.

"Actress Ruth Gordon always said, 'Never face facts,' but we must face them. The facts are these. . . ."

"I think you'll agree that the time for selfishness is past. Each one of us must put aside some time to serve our country, whether in the armed forces or in some alternative service. As John Kennedy said, 'Ask not what your country can do for you, ask what you can do for your country.' "

Ask for action. If it's appropriate to your topic, use your close to ask your audience to act.

"Now is the time to tell our school board how we feel about drug testing. At tomorrow's meeting, speak out against these procedures. Speak out in favor of freedom."

Finish with an anecdote. Any story you use to close should bring together the main points of your speech. Make up one that's appropriate.

Go out with optimism. Tell your audience why you think things are getting better, or why there will be peace, or why you expect sales to rise.

"Female athletes will not stop until all professional doors are open. Right now there's a woman on the Harlem Globetrotters; it's only a matter of time until there's a woman wearing Yankee pinstripes."

Close with a question. A strong rhetorical question—that is, a question to which you don't expect an answer—can make an effective ending to a speech.

"If professional baseball players, many of whom are known offenders, can refuse drug testing, should we as innocent students be forced to be tested against our will?"

"Female athletes are as strong, as swift, and as skilled as their male counterparts. Why should they be denied, on the basis of gender alone, the challenges and reward of playing professional ball?"

Once you have written a complete draft of your speech, put it aside for a time, and then begin the process of revision.

WORKING FROM FIRST DRAFT

6

In composing, as a general rule, run your pen through every other word you have written; you have no idea what vigor it will give your style.

Sydney Smith

Now that you have created a complete draft of your speech, you are ready to begin the process of revision. No matter how tempted you are to skip this step, don't. Your first draft may contain all your best ideas about your subject, but your revised draft will contain those ideas in a way that makes them easily available to your audience. Never deliver the first draft of a speech.

Revising always takes more time than you think it will or should. "Revise" means "to see again." It implies that you have seen your draft once, you have stopped seeing it, and you have gone back to look at it afresh.

LET IT COOL

The "stop seeing it" part is sometimes hard to arrange, especially if you are working on short deadlines or if you've left writing your speech to the last minute.

But you will need time away from your draft in order to be able to revise it. Allow at least a night's sleep to intervene between finishing the first draft and beginning the process of revision, if you can possibly arrange it. If not, give yourself a few hours of a different kind of activity. It's best to do something that does not involve words: go for a walk or listen to music.

CUTTING

I write long, and my revisions always start with cutting out the excess words, sentences, and paragraphs that obscure rather than add to my meaning. Cutting is an important step. By its nature, writing is an imprecise process. We tend to use the "scaffolding" of excess language as an aid to getting what we really mean down on the paper.

Once the meaning is out, though, and the "house" of the speech is erected, the scaffolding must come down. That's what cutting is for. You no doubt needed those extra words, clauses, sentences, paragraphs, pages, when you were writing, or they wouldn't be there. But your audience doesn't need to hear how you arrived at your statement, only the statement itself. The more clear, succinct, simple, direct, and compelling you can make that statement during revision, the more easily your audience will hear, appreciate, absorb, and react to it. So get your red or blue pencil ready and cut out everything you don't really need.

*". . . which brings us to
the end of 1947—and I hear
you asking yourself—how
about 1948!"*
[Get to the point!]

"I've taken all the weak
spots out of your speech,
Senator. We're left with,
'Ladies and gentlemen. . .
thank you!' "

First, go through every sentence of your draft and cut all unnecessary words. You'll recognize them. Some are easy to spot: *really*, *very*, *sort of*, *kind of*, and so on. Look, too, for the weasel words: words that soften your meaning, cloud it, make it fuzzy or less than clear. These include *try* (as in the sentence, "We are going to try to do something about it"), *probably*, *maybe*, and others.

Then there are the loose adjectives, like *nice* and *pretty*. Get rid of these altogether. If they leave a gaping hole, find a sharper adjective: do you mean *striking*, *smashing*, or *lovely* instead of nice? A thesaurus is helpful here, but don't get carried away.

In speaking, use words that the ear can hear easily. This means you should avoid words you can't pronounce, words that sound like other words (such as *boy* and *buoy*) and words that are too fancy for the surrounding language. A word like *effulgent*, for example, will probably only be appropriate once in a lifetime. In most cases, *bright* will do.

After you've cut the extra words, look for phrases or clauses you don't need. Then consider cutting whole sentences. Have you said the same thing twice, in two different ways, in two separate sentences? Try your speech with one, then the other sentence. Does either work better, or do you need to combine the best parts of each to create a new sentence that says exactly what you mean?

DOES IT MAKE SENSE?

Now that you have cut out all excess, go through the speech again and make notes next to each paragraph in the margin, stating the point of each paragraph in a few words. Then reread just these summaries in order.

Do your ideas flow and develop logically? Does the

speech add up? Have you left anything out? If so, write and insert the additional material.

Look at the entire speech again. Do your transitions work well? Have you provided your listeners with guideposts they can hear? These are words like *first*, *second*, and *third*, when you are making three points, or words like *to begin*, *next*, and *finally*. These guideposts help your audience know where they are in your speech. Smooth out these and all other connections.

By now you probably think you are through. You have examined words, phrases, clauses, sentences, and paragraphs, and tested each one against the questions: Do I need it? Does it add to my listeners' understanding of my main point, or does it confuse the issue?

But there is one final thing to look for. Is there a phrase, a sentence, a paragraph, a page, that you just love? Some piece of language that seems to stand out from the rest as your best work, your favorite part? Trust me and Samuel Johnson, who said, "Read over your compositions, and, when you meet a passage which you think is particularly fine, strike it out."

Not that it isn't good writing—it probably is, but if it stands out that clearly, it doesn't belong in your speech. It may eventually belong in another speech; it may become a poem, a short story, a letter to your aunt. But take it out of the speech.

WRITING FOR THE EAR

Now that you have cut out all the flab, gotten rid of the scaffolding, checked your transitions and the flow of your ideas, take a look, or rather a listen, to what's left.

Read your speech out loud. To yourself. Alone. You don't need a tape recorder for this. You must pay attention to the way you feel when you read your speech.

Do the words flow easily, or do you get stuck as words pile up together? Are there too many "s" sounds, so that you feel like a hissing snake as you speak? Or do the words thump along, with no particularly musical rhythm? Have you taken out too many transitional phrases, and do you now need to add some back in? Make whatever changes you must so that the speech fits your voice.

Think, too, of simplifying your language so that your audience can get your meaning as they hear your words. There is a big difference between the printed page, which you have before you and can look at again and again, and words spoken into the air, moving past inexorably. Your audience will not be able to go back and listen again to what you just said if they didn't understand it the first time. And if they lose the flow of your ideas, they are likely to become bored and restless.

Make your speech so easy to follow, so lucid and clear that your audience will recall point A when you get to point C.

Here are some suggestions you might consider:

Use short, simple words rather than long, complicated words.

Original	Revision
initiate	start
exemplify	show
utilize	use
reprimand	scold
conflagration	fire

Use parallel construction.

Original: He came, he saw, and the city was conquered.

Revision: **He came, he saw, he conquered.**

Group your ideas in threes. For some reason, the ear readily hears words, phrases, and clauses that appear in groups of three.

Whether it's baseball, basketball, or ballet, get some exercise daily.

". . . of the people, by the people, for the people . . ."

It's up to parents, it's up to students, and it's up to administrators to stop this blatant abuse of justice.

Pair elements you wish to compare or contrast.

"Ask not what your country can do for you, ask what you can do for your country."

On the one hand, women in the major leagues sounds shocking; on the other hand, it makes sense.

Either colored pencils or marking pens can be used to give your finished sketch more color.

Use short, simple sentences for emphasis.

I wish I could tell you there is an easy cure. I can't. There isn't.

Repeat key words or phrases you wish to emphasize.

Perennials are beautiful. Perennials are hardy. Perennials are easy to maintain. Why not begin planning your own perennial garden now?

Repeat sounds to create interest and link your thoughts. Note the repeated use of "un" in the sentences below.

Drug testing is unfair. Drug testing is un-American. And drug testing is unreliable.

FITTING INTO YOUR TIME LIMIT

When you picked your topic, you scaled it to your time limit, of course, but now you read your speech aloud and time it. And you find that your draft is either too long or too short. What to do?

First, respect the limit. There's rarely an excuse for speaking much less or much longer than expected, although a minute or two either way probably won't matter. If your speech is too short, you may be tempted to invoke the example of Abraham Lincoln and the Gettysburg Address, which was much shorter than anyone expected and is a model of oratory.

Remember, however, that your situation may not be as fortunate as Mr. Lincoln's. Maybe the marching band is getting into position or someone is changing costumes or pouring coffee during the time allotted for your speech. Or perhaps your teacher has specified a fifteen-minute speech, and will grade you down—no matter how excellent your presentation—if you don't follow instructions to the letter.

Whatever the case, here are some strategies for working with your draft until it fits the time you've got to fill.

HOW TO SHORTEN A SPEECH

You've already cut every extra word, clause, phrase, sentence, and paragraph. You've removed pages of excess. You can still cut more.

"Strict rule.
None of the speeches
are over fifteen minutes."

Now you are not going to be involved with removing the words that make your ideas cloudy; you are going to remove or simplify some of the ideas.

Go back over your outline and see what you can afford to give up. Be prepared to find some psychic resistance to giving up anything, but be firm. Something has to go.

Usually, some minor point can be disposed of without doing real damage to the speech. You may have given four reasons why drug testing is a bad idea; perhaps you can manage with three or combine two into one. Or maybe an idea you've spent an entire paragraph developing can be treated in a single sentence, or made into a phrase that fits inside another sentence. Be careful when doing this kind of telescoping that the language and structure don't become convoluted and difficult to listen to.

Be prepared to give up some of your subtlety or complexity. It is better to say a few things clearly and well than to say everything you know about a subject and have nothing remembered.

HOW TO LENGTHEN
A SPEECH

Suppose you've taken out all the excess language, cleared up all fuzziness of thought, and you find yourself with a speech that's short of what's required—whether by three or four minutes, or more.

You may be tempted to put the padding back in, a "really" here, a "very" there, to add a few extra adjectives or an adverb collection. You may be tempted to say the same thing twice.

Don't. There are ways to lengthen a speech. The trick is to add new information, fresh thought, not just words.

Elaborate. Look back over your draft. Are there

places where you can explain in more detail just what you're talking about? For example, if you've said, "There are nine players on a baseball team," you could then list the positions. You could say that only nine team members are fielded during the game, but that the team is actually a much larger entity, and list all the people, including owners, managers, etc., who comprise a team. The important thing is to add information that is interesting and useful to the audience.

Add quotes. Adding a relevant quote or two is another way to lengthen a speech. Consult a source such as *Peter's Quotations*, and read around in a few topic areas. For instance, in your speech about drug testing, you might consult Education, Force, Freedom and Liberty, or Youth. You might find just the quote that will give you a stronger opening and a bridge into the main body of your speech, a quote that raises an issue you haven't thought of before and would like to address, a quote that will help you close your speech in an extra paragraph or two, really sending the audience off with something pithy to think about.

Insert anecdotes. Make up a story to drive one of your points home. In a speech about the importance of brand names, for example, one writer created several fictitious computer companies to make her point:

> You go into a local computer store and say, "I'm in the market for a personal computer." And the salesman shows you a Widget 180, a personal-sized WingDing, and a compact desk-model Numbercruncher Deluxe.

> Depending on the kind of person you are, you may or may not ask to see an IBM computer. But you will certainly wonder why the salesman isn't showing you one. Everyone who thinks computer thinks IBM first, except this guy. Maybe he makes a bigger commission on the

Widget 180, you think, or maybe he's unloading Numbercrunchers because the company is going under—or maybe he just doesn't know his business. You decide to shop elsewhere.

Come up with a new angle. Try to imagine how some character in history would respond to your speech: "Give me liberty or give me death"? How someone from another country would respond: "In Russia, we would send you to Siberia for even thinking about marijuana"? How would your mother respond? An alien from outer space? Answers to questions like these can often give you additional ideas.

Yes, but . . . Imagining an objection to what you've written can also give you ideas. You can either try to think up objections or read your speech to a friend or parent and ask your audience to play devil's advocate. They may be able to come up with some objections you haven't considered. Build these objections into your speech, along with your responses to them, of course, and your speech will not only be longer, it will be stronger, too.

ADDITIONAL REMEDIES

You've cut the fluff. You've made your speech easy to read and easy to listen to. It fits your time limit to the second. But there's still something wrong with it. What then?

If it's dull. Try making the language more colorful and specific. Use concrete nouns and active verbs. Give clear examples instead of generalities. Adding quotes, statistics, and facts will bring abstractions to life.

Original: **The kind of exercise you do is less important than how often you do it.**

Revision: **Pick basketball, or badminton, or ballet. But whatever form of exercise you choose, do it regularly—for at least thirty minutes each session, three times each week.**

Tinker with rhythms and sentence structure. Use sound patterns, like the three "b" words in the example above, to enliven the writing for your listeners.

Underline the sections of your speech that you find most interesting. How are they different from the parts you consider dull? What can you do to improve the less interesting parts, bringing them up to the level of the best?

One word of caution: your speech may be less dull than you think it is. Maybe you've worked on it too long, and too hard, to the point where you can't tell what's interesting and what's not. Ask an honest and compassionate friend's opinion.

If it sounds too simple. Be careful. Simple is often good. Don't confuse simple with stupid. True simplicity, and the clarity that goes with it, are very difficult to achieve—and worth struggling for. Don't succumb to the temptation to make things sound more complex than they are.

But if you think your speech really does sound too simple, perhaps it's your sentence structure. Do most of your sentences follow the subject-verb-object pattern? Introduce a little variety.

If it's too complicated. Go back to step 1 of the speechwriting process. Ask yourself, What one thing am I trying to say? Make sure every sentence and paragraph adds something and helps convey that main thought. Simplify sentence structure. Use easier words.

After each difficult sentence, ask yourself, What do I mean? How can I say this in other words? Write those other words down: they probably say, simply, exactly, what you want your audience to know.

If your speech is full of complicated information, though, you may want to consider using visual aids to help your audience grasp in one quick look what words seem to take forever to explain.

USING
VISUAL AIDS

7

Everyone knows a picture is worth at least a thousand words, which explains why most business and professional speakers today travel with a carousel, or two, or three, of slides to accompany their speeches.

These slides almost certainly include a number of charts and graphs. They might show the growth of sales in dollars and units, or this year's profits versus last year's, or how many widgets the U.S. Widget Company has to manufacture to stay even.

Word slides are also popular. You might see "Sell, sell, sell" in increasingly large letters, highlighted with neon and rainbow effects. A slide could show a list of the magazines where the company's newest ads will run, or the four steps store managers can take to cut shrinkage, or ten ways to stop waste.

Sometimes, of course, the slides show pictures. These might be faces of target customers, shots of ads used in the new campaign, or magazine covers arranged in a graceful fan. Pictures of new products, manufacturing facilities or processes, even political or satirical cartoons, might appear on slides to accompany a speech.

Unless you are speaking about your trip to Greece or giving a talk on a subject such as art history or architecture, for which premade slides are readily available, slides such as those used by professional and business speakers will probably be out of the question for you. They can be time-consuming and costly to produce.

Nevertheless, the speechmaker's use of visual aids can be adapted to your needs. Simpler technologies, including flip charts, blackboards, and overhead projectors, can help you add visual interest when it's your turn at the podium.

Visuals are obviously inappropriate for certain speaking occasions. You probably wouldn't use a flip chart if you're delivering the valedictory address on a topic such as the value of being true to yourself. On the other hand, some topics cry out for illustration. Travel, fine art, gardening—in short, the highly visual subjects—may be difficult to address without the help of pictures.

Most occasions, however, fall somewhere in between. You will have to judge whether or not visuals are appropriate additions to your speech.

DO I NEED VISUAL AIDS?

Before you try to decide how you will present your graphics to an audience, first determine whether visuals will add anything to your speech. Read through your revised text, looking for places where a picture would be appropriate.

Are there spots where you use a great many words to explain a statistic that could easily be illustrated? Are you presenting many statistics which when read aloud

*Visual aids are useful,
though the map would be
hard to see by an audience.*

are difficult to relate to each other but when pictured become immediately clear?

Are any of your quotes from sources that were originally visual, such as captions from cartoons? Does it take many words to explain the visual, and then is the impact lost?

Is there any person, place, or thing that must be shown for the audience to understand your subject.?

Would illustrations make understanding easier? Or would they just be window dressing, nice but not really necessary?

Adding visuals to a dull or poorly written speech will not improve it, and no one will be fooled. Words are the basic building blocks of speeches, and words come first. Only when words prove inadequate because of the nature of the subject—not the ability of the writer—should pictures be called on to help.

If you decide you need pictures to go with some of your words, don't sprinkle your illustrations, one here, one there, throughout your speech. Isolate them into a single area: for instance, you might include charts of statistics showing the rise of drug use among teenagers at the beginning of your speech. Your audience will still be fresh enough to absorb them, and, once your facts are established, you can leave the visuals behind and go on to your arguments and conclusions.

Sometimes, just thinking about visualizing a speech can help tighten an already good draft. It's an exercise worth trying. For each paragraph, write a word or phrase that you want your audience to remember, and an appropriate illustration. For example,

- Teenage drug usage on the rise—chart
- Response of law enforcement agencies—photo of law officers
- What parents can do—three steps
- Why drug testing in high schools won't work— four reasons

After you've done this, consider whether you really need the pictures or whether you can create the picture you need or want with language. For instance, talk about the *dramatic rise* of drug usage, rather than using a chart. Create a word picture of drug arrest procedures. Say at the beginning of the section, "There are three steps parents can take . . . " and then use the words *First*, *Second*, and *Third* to introduce each step. Do the same with "four reasons."

There are two more points to consider. First, if your speech is for class, check with your teacher that it's okay to use visual aids. Second, make sure the equipment you plan to use will be available. Don't assume there will be a blackboard or an easel or an overhead projector. Plan ahead. Ask.

VISUAL AIDS TO CONSIDER

Suppose you have read through your speech, marked and grouped all the visuals, and decided that you do want to illustrate some of your material. What kinds of aids are available? Consider the following:

Blackboards

Good teachers know the value of this simple tool. Blackboards are widely available, fun and easy to use, cheap, and very effective when they are used well.

When using a blackboard, write only the most important words. Remember, you want to emphasize key points. Plan what you will write ahead of time, working it out on paper if need be.

Be sure to write legibly. Better yet, print. Write large, using your whole arm. Press firmly on the chalk.

You can write more than words on a blackboard. Drawings and diagrams can be very helpful. When talking about a football play, the history of an idea, or the logic of a computer program, you can use the blackboard to help make your points.

Flip Charts

If you like the idea of a chalkboard but one isn't available, you can use a flip chart to much the same effect. You will need a pad of large paper, at least 14 by 17 inches, an easel to stand it on, and some broad-tipped markers.

The key item in this list is the easel. You can't draw and hold a large pad of paper at the same time. And there's no satisfactory substitute for an easel. Makeshift propping will end with your visual on the floor and you in a frenzy. If you can't get an easel, use a different visual format or none at all.

You can use a flip chart in three ways: Preprinted, prepared, or written on the spot.

Preprinted means just that: you draw your charts, graphs, maps or write out your key words and phrases on the pages before you speak. This tends to give the effect of speaking from notes if you aren't careful. It does, however, provide a way to jog your memory if you are unsure about the structure of your speech.

A slight variation of the preprinted approach is to prepare your flip charts ahead of time, but instead of using dark markers, write out your points and sketch in your charts very lightly in pencil. While you are speaking, you merely go over the light writing you have done with a marker. Your words and diagrams become visible to the audience; it appears as if you are creating the charts as you go.

While this method is safe, it can also be dull. You must be careful not to look as if you are writing over something that's already there; you must practice using your marker as if your thoughts are flowing as your arm is moving.

The third way of using a flip chart, writing on it as you speak, assures spontaneity. Speakers who create flip charts as they go along seem—and usually are—exceptionally confident and in control. They have good memories; they don't forget what they meant to write or draw midspeech. If you're shaky about your memory, it's best to prepare your flipcharts ahead of time.

Overhead Projectors

Overhead projectors are available in many schools. The information to be presented is on a plastic sheet, or transparency, which is laid on a glass plate on the projector. A light shines through the transparency, and the image it contains is magnified through an overhead glass and projected on a screen in the front of the room.

While overhead projectors can be effective tools, remember that transparencies must be prepared ahead of time. You can do this either by writing on them with grease pencil or by having them prepared from typed documents through your school's audiovisual technician.

Remember that overhead projectors, like slides, must be used in darkened rooms. For many people, darkness equals sleep. It's easier to lose your audience's attention when the lights are low. If you use an overhead, be sure both you and your visuals are compelling.

Show and Tell

Sometimes the best visual is the thing itself. If you're discussing an article in *Time* magazine, bring in the issue and quote from it. If you're talking about how shoes are made, you might point to parts of an actual shoe as you detail each process.

The "show and tell" technique works best with a small audience in a fairly small room, one in which it is possible for everyone to see clearly the object you are holding up. If the exhibit you bring in isn't large enough to be seen when you hold it up to discuss it, read from it, or use it as a prop, don't bring it.

MAKING INFORMATION VISUAL

Now that you have selected your medium, decide how you will put your information into visual form.

Words

Whether you're using a blackboard, a flip chart, or overheads, you can use words as visuals to make your points and help your audience remember what you are saying. Use as few words as possible, and make sure the ones you choose are hard-hitting, expressing the kernel of your thought concisely, in a memorable way.

If you are making a list, use parallel construction and the same size lettering for items of similar importance.

For example, suppose you want to use words to emphasize to your audience the three main reasons you feel drug testing of students by the school board would be unfair. You might use the following words:

Right:

DRUG TESTING IS UNFAIR BECAUSE:
all students are equally suspect
test results are not accurate
constitutional rights are violated

Wrong:

Drug testing is unfair because:
ALL STUDENTS ARE EQUALLY SUSPECT
Inaccuracy of results
violation of CONSTITUTIONAL RIGHTS

Maps

Whether you are describing your trip through Italy, detailing Washington's march on Trenton, or showing the size of the United States before and after the Loui-

Dr. Helen Caldicott, a well-known antinuclear activist, holding a very appropriate "prop" for a Mother's Day demonstration against war.

siana Purchase, a map can help. In fact, when you need a map, nothing else will really do.

Unfortunately, most maps aren't big enough to be seen from more than a foot away. If they are, they may be too big to hold. Use pushpins to tack a map up to a wall if your audience will be able to see it. Otherwise, you can draw a map in chalk on the blackboard or in pen on a flip chart or overhead transparency. These sketches will of course be rough, but they can help you demonstrate movement across a country, for example, or the proximity of a city to the sea.

Charts and Graphs
Numerical information which is muddied up by language can become readily accessible when you use a chart or graph.

Consider these examples.

Words without chart

"Now I'd like to talk about our sales in relation to profits for 1986 versus 1985. In 1985, we sold 4.2 million widgets and made a profit of $1,260,000. In 1986, we sold 4.5 million widgets but our profit was only $1,240,000.

"Obviously, our sales to profit ratio has declined. We are making only 27.5 percent profit in 1986, while we made 30 percent profit in 1985. We are selling more widgets, but we are making less money."

Words with chart

	1985	1986
Sales units	4.2 million	4.5 million
Profits	$1.26 million	$1.24 million
Profit/sales ratio	30.0%	27.5%

"As you can see, though our sales have increased slightly during the past year, our profits have declined rather dramatically. We are selling more widgets, but we are making less money."

Even the simplest chart can help you to eliminate some fairly confusing language while it enables you to present information clearly and concisely.

Many charts and graphs are easy to do and can be drawn on the board, on a flip chart, or on a transparency for an overhead. Here are some of the most useful kinds of charts and graphs.

Tables. The example above is actually a table, that is, a short, neatly arranged list of various items, as a table of contents.

Keep tables simple; don't try to include too much information. In the example above, for instance, you might include one more line (sales in dollars, for example) or one more column (another year's results). More than that, however, and the table would be too cluttered to be really useful.

Also, be sure your numbers line up. Keep decimal points under one another. If you are adding or subtracting numbers in a column, be absolutely sure your mathematics are correct.

Line graphs. Line graphs are the classic graphs shown on the back wall in business cartoons. They feature jagged lines that shoot up and fall down, forming what look like peaks and valleys; some dips and rises are steeper than others.

Line graphs are excellent for showing changes in quantity over time, whether sales, profits, production, births, deaths, whatever. The bottom axis, the horizontal, always indicates time. You may divide it up as you like: days, months, years, even centuries. Just be certain you use the same unit of time all the way across and that the divisions are equal.

The vertical axis, on the left-hand side, is used to indicate quantities. Again, be sure increments are even, and do not include more information than your audience can handle. At most, you can graph two quantities on the same line graph. If you need to show more, use a separate graph. The point is to make the information clear, not to jam as much onto one visual as possible.

Bar charts. Bar charts are useful for showing comparisons between quantities. You might use a bar chart to show how many cars were sold versus how many trucks, year by year, for several years. The bars can be horizontal or vertical.

Again, don't put too much information on a single chart. Your audience needs only a snapshot of the relationship of one quantity to another, not a documentary. Keep it simple.

Pictures

If you can get good, large-size photos of what you wish to illustrate, by all means use them. You need something that can be seen from a distance. Oversized glossy magazines such as *Life* are good sources for photos showing damage done to burn victims, the effects of a hurricane, the size of a crowd gathered to greet a hero, and so on.

Videotapes

Many business and professional speakers use video clips—three- to five-minute segments of videotape—to illustrate their points or present information. If video playback equipment will be available and if your audience is small, fifteen to twenty people at most, you can show a short segment of videotape as part of your speech. You might want to show a segment from a television sitcom, for example, about drug usage, or show some slow-motion footage of two or three major league hitters for a talk on batting styles.

If you do show a tape, be sure to introduce it and to transition away from it effectively. Let your audience know what they are going to see. ("Now I'm going to show you a brief videotape of X, Y, and Z at the plate.") And be sure you let your audience know how the tape relates to what you are talking about. ("You'll see a variety of stances here, illustrating my point that there's more than one way to swing a bat.")

After the tape, connect back to your topic. ("I think you'll agree that today's sitcoms, though they are dealing with the issue of drug usage, aren't really taking a hard-line approach.")

Remember, speeches are made of words—spoken words, not images. None of the techniques for enlivening a speech with visuals will make a bad speech good. But a creative and correct use of visuals can be like the salt on the potato chips—that little something that adds a lot. They can help your audience both understand and remember your message better. They can make the difference between just okay and excellent.

PRACTICING YOUR DELIVERY

8

Think of your speech as a baseball. Now imagine the perfect pitch. It's on time and on target. It does exactly what the pitcher wants it to do. Whether it's high, wide, inside, fast, or slow, it's under control.

You'll want that much command over the delivery of your speech. You'll want to have enough control over both your text and your voice to be able to slow down, speed up, emphasize forcefully, or soften what you're saying with a gesture. To get that level of major league command, you'll need to practice. You'll have to be willing to say your speech again and again until you can put it exactly where it belongs every time, as if it were second nature.

How much will you need to practice? Lots. One successful corporate executive who speaks regularly says a new speech requires ten times as long to practice as it takes to give. That means for every half hour of speaking, she will spend five hours practicing her delivery.

President John F. Kennedy, an impressive speaker, using body language to make a point during a speech on medical care for the aged in 1962.

Now she's a fast-track type, a driven perfectionist, so you may need a little less time than that. But assume that you will need to practice your delivery at least three times as long as you will speak, and the more, the better—up to a limit of ten.

Can you practice too much? Some people say yes, and I am inclined to agree. Rehearsing your speech a thousand times before your actual performance could take all the fun out of it for you. On the other hand, not enough practice might leave you with a bad case of stage fright and no rehearsal skills to fall back on. And to be honest, few people have practiced their delivery to the point of dullness.

Even if you've gone over your speech a hundred times, it's new when you stand before the audience because the situation is different. There's that extra lift, the exciting edge you get from being "on." If you've practiced well, you'll be able to take that energy and put it to use. If you haven't, that surge of adrenalin may overwhelm you. Decide to practice.

First, be sure the text of your speech or your note cards are ready. Prepare the materials you will use when you stand up to speak. What you need depends on whether you will be reading your speech, speaking from note cards, or working from memory.

PREPARING A TYPED SPEECH FOR READING

Reading from a prepared text, either typed pages or a teleprompter, is preferred by business speakers and politicians. It provides a clear, unambiguous set of things to say. It takes the pressure off remembering and puts the emphasis on delivery. If at all possible, try to read your speech from a prepared text.

Type your speech double or triple spaced. Use wide margins, at least 2 inches on both the right- and the left-hand sides. Make sure you mark paragraphs, so you know where a new thought begins. I find it better to skip an extra space or two rather than to indent. It's easier for the eye, and reminds you to breathe between paragraphs.

Use capitals and lowercase letters when you type, rather than all caps. Again, this makes it easier for your eye to know when a sentence begins. If you have access to a typewriter or printer with a large typeface, such as Orator, by all means use it.

Be sure to spell out everything just as you will say it. If you are going to say "three hundred and eighty-six students were tested," spell out the number rather than typing 386. Your eye and tongue may not coordinate when faced with numbers in the midst of words.

Spell out abbreviations, too, just as you intend to say them. Say "Equal Rights Amendment" the first time it appears. Afterwards, you may use the abbreviated form, E.R.A., but when typing be sure to use capital letters and put periods between them. Otherwise you may find yourself saying "era."

Remove as many stumbling blocks as possible from your prepared script. Remember that you will be (however slightly) nervous. Make your speech as simple for your eye as possible.

Finally, number your pages in the top right-hand corner. Should your speech come apart on your way to the stage, you will be able to put it in order again quickly.

PREPARING SPEAKER'S NOTES OR OUTLINE

Speaking from notes or an outline can be very effective, especially if you are a naturally articulate person who has no trouble finding words or putting them together into coherent sentences.

Build your outline or notes from the draft you've prepared. Go through what you've written and underline the topic sentences. Then number the subsidiary or supporting points. Mark key phrases, spots where the language is precise and important. Unless you are a gifted natural speaker, your written phrases are probably better than what you'll think up on your feet. Make sure your best writing makes it to your speaking outline or note cards: you don't want it to go to waste.

Whether you prepare a one- or two-page outline or put your main thoughts onto index cards is up to you. Sheets have the advantage of being less likely to scatter across the floor just as you advance to the speaker's platform. Cards, whether 3 by 5 inches or 4 by 6 inches, may seem less conspicuous than sheets of paper, and looking through them as you speak will give you something to do with your hands.

Type or print your outline or notes plainly on one side of the paper or note cards. Make sure that they are easy to read. Leave enough space so that you can add additional points or phrases if they come up as you practice. Number your pages or cards boldly at the top.

MEMORIZING

Both the prepared text and the cards described above can be useful to the speaker who has to memorize.

First, memorize your outline. Think of it as getting the skeleton of your speech into place. Then memorize the language you need to flesh it out. Once you understand and know the flow of ideas, it will be easier to hold the words you want to use in mind.

Unless you are delivering a speech written by someone else, or your teacher is holding a copy of your text and checking your memory against it, only you will know the words you are supposed to be saying. And only you will know if you miss one or two, or change a phrase here and there midspeech. Keep your outline in mind; ultimately, it is more useful to you than the exact words you've written. If you forget a few words you can always move on to the next point of the outline, but if you forget your line of reasoning, the logical development of your argument, you can be in real trouble.

YOUR VOICE

Now that your text, outline, or cards are ready, set them aside for a few moments, and pay attention to your voice.

How does your throat feel? How does it feel when you think about standing up in front of a group and delivering your speech? How does it feel when you open your mouth and begin to speak?

Chances are, when you think about speaking, or when you begin, your throat will feel tight. Just a little, or maybe a lot. How relaxed your throat is will influence the quality of your voice: whether it sounds warm and melodious or tight and frightened.

The best thing you can do for your voice, and your delivery in general, is to relax. Don't try to cough or clear your throat. Those actions will only tense your throat muscles further. Instead, take a sip of water—not too cold—swallow it, inhale deeply and exhale, mouth open, letting your jaw drop. Pick up your speech, outline, or note cards and begin to speak, pretending you are in front of the group.

Now, try to really listen to yourself. How does your voice sound? If it's controlled, warm, and easy—fine. If you don't like what you hear, check each of the points that follow.

Posture. Are you standing straight? Is your neck straight? It's easier to produce a good tone if you are standing correctly. Even tilting your head to the side slightly or bending forward too far to look at your notes can put a strain on your throat. Don't stand like a general, but stand tall, straighten your head as you let your shoulders drop.

Can you breathe freely? Voice is produced by air passing through the larynx, and it follows that the more freely and easily you can breathe, the more easily you will speak. Loosen your collar and tie, remove that choker, let your belt out a notch or two and breathe.

Remember that it's difficult to breathe easily just after a big meal. Eat lightly before practicing and especially before performance.

Here are some exercises that will help to relax you so that you can speak more easily:

Yawn, or move your mouth as if you were yawning. Tilt your head back as you do. Feel your throat muscles loosen.

Rotate your head slowly forward, right, back, left, then around the opposite way.

Bend forward from the waist, shake out your hands and arms from the shoulder, and sway loosely. Be Raggedy Ann or Andy for a moment. Then stand up straight. Breathe deeply, exhale.

Now, begin reading your speech. This is no time to criticize your writing. Major revisions should be unnecessary at this point; you've revised carefully already. You may need to make minor word changes if you find what you've written is difficult to pronounce or if it sounds odd to your ear when you read it. If you're speaking from notes, you may want to jot down a fortuitous phrase that occurs to you during practice so you'll remember it at the podium. You may rearrange phrases for better rhythm, but resist the impulse to do major rewrites. Just read.

Here are some things to pay attention to:

Speed. Many people talk too fast when they get nervous. Other people can't seem to get their words out at all. Practice reading slowly. And then more slowly. Then read a little faster. Knowing you can control the rate at which you read will be very helpful when that first rush of adrenalin hits you at the podium.

Practice varying speeds throughout the speech to give it texture. Convey your meaning by careful pacing, pausing at commas, breathing at the ends of sentences. You may want to mark significant pauses, or places where you need to take a breath, right in your text.

Emphasis. Emphasize important words, underlining them with your voice, so that your meaning will be clear to your audience. Put the weight of your voice where it will do the most good. A shift in emphasis can reinforce or change a meaning. Consider the difference emphasis subtle shifts can make in this quote from Abraham Lincoln:

> If the *good* people, in *their* wisdom, shall see fit to keep *me* in the background, I have been *too familiar* with disappointments to be very *much* chagrined.

> If the good *people,* in their *wisdom*, shall *see fit* to keep me in the *background*, I have been too familiar with *disappointments* to be very much *chagrined.*

The first version places more emphasis on the speaker's differentiation between them (the good people) and me (the speaker). The second version places the emphasis—more correctly—on how the speaker will feel if he is not elected.

OTHER ASPECTS OF SPEAKING

If you find yourself gasping for breath, shorten your sentences or mark pauses in your prepared script.

If you are saying "em" and "eh" between words, remember that these verbal tics will interfere with your meaning. Your audience may start paying more attention to these extra sounds than to your message.

Speak clearly. Pronounce all the words. Don't slur over syllables.

Speak loudly. Practice projecting, as actors call it, directing your voice so that it can be heard clearly at a distance.

It may take two or three readings until you are comfortable with your delivery and have marked your text to indicate where to slow down, speed up, or emphasize. These variations will give life and color to your presentation. You might find it helpful to make notes on a photocopy of your text as you work out the dynamics of your speech. Then you can transfer only the marks you really need to the copy you'll speak from.

After you've marked your speech, read it aloud to yourself two or three times, just to get the sound of it. Then try reading to a mirror. You can practice eye contact and work out gestures. Use your hands and your head and your whole posture as necessary to reinforce what your words are saying. Lean forward for emphasis. Lift one hand, then the other, as you state opposing sides of an argument.

When you've finished working with a mirror, read your speech to someone you know: friend, parent, brother or sister—anyone who will listen. Practice making eye contact, and put in all the emphasis, gestures, pacing, and so on, that you've already rehearsed alone.

This audience can't take its
eyes off actress/comedienne
Whoopi Goldberg.

If you make a mistake, keep going. You want to practice the total speech, not just a portion. Besides, you need to work out what you'll do when you skip a line or mispronounce a word.

FEEDBACK

Of course, you will ask your practice audience what they think of your speech. You hope they will say, "That's the best speech I ever heard. You were wonderful."

But what if they are more critical than that? Don't be defensive. You want to learn. You want to improve. Listen to what they have to say.

Be sure you listen to more than their words. Your audience may not know how to tell you what really needs improvement. Usually, however, they can point you toward the places that need work. Ask questions, trying to get your listeners to pinpoint just what bothered them, if anything. If Aunt Essie says the beginning was too weak, does she mean what you said, or how you said it, or both?

Have confidence in yourself. Ultimately, you have to decide whether to go with the ending as it stands or alter it somewhat because three people you read it to said it didn't work for them. Listen to comments patiently, evaluate them calmly, and decide whether they're useful. If they are, make changes. If not, forget them.

Besides what your listeners say, pay attention to their body language as you speak. Are they looking at you attentively? Fidgeting? Nodding and yawning? Try to read the subtle messages they are giving you. Making a speech is a kind of dialogue, but what the audience says is usually communicated without words. Learning to listen to it will make you a better speaker.

If they are nodding in agreement, you know you're doing well.

If they are yawning, the room may be stuffy or you may not be speaking loudly or clearly enough. You may not have enough variety in your pitch or pacing. A sing-song or monotone will put people to sleep faster than Brahms' "Lullaby."

What if the audience seems restless or shuffling? These are signs that they are not engaged. You need to hook up with them again. Are you speaking loudly enough? Are you pronouncing your words clearly? Enunciating? Are you making eye contact? Try stepping forward, speaking up, animating your gestures.

PRACTICING WITH TAPE RECORDERS AND VIDEO EQUIPMENT

After you've read your speech to several people, you may want to read it into a tape recorder or have a friend videotape a practice session. Try to read to people first, though, before you turn to technology. It's helpful to have audience reactions to test against your performance on tape. Now you are ready to listen to, and perhaps to watch, your speech as another person would. You are ready to judge whether what Aunt Essie said about your opening makes sense, and whether or not the ending needs a more emphatic delivery.

Read your speech to the tape recorder or camera as you've practiced it. Now play it back. Don't be surprised if you don't sound or look like yourself. No one does. The shock wears off quickly, however, if you just keep listening and/or watching.

Here are some hints on rehearsing with audio and videotape.

Working with a Tape Recorder
Play back your entire speech, and listen without looking at your text or notes or outline. Follow the ideas. Do

they make sense? Are transitions clear? Do the thoughts flow logically? Does your voice shift to accommodate changes in thought and to emphasize important meanings? Is your voice interesting to listen to, varied, controlled? Do your pauses heighten your meaning? Is your speech free of the clutter of "ehs," "ers," and "ems"?

After one listen through, listen again, this time with text in hand. What is the best thing about your reading? How can you get more of that? Are there any changes you should make based on how the speech sounds? Is there anything you can write on the text to remind you to do something well or to improve? Make comments on your typescript; then read the speech to the tape recorder again and listen to how you've improved.

Working with Video
If you're lucky enough to have someone who can videotape your practice, go ahead. Don't be distracted by how you look on tape. Begin by just listening, eyes closed, to your delivery. Follow the suggestions given above for improving delivery when using audiotape.

Next, watch the tape without sound. How do you look? Bored? Anxious? Tired? Or do you seem relaxed, animated, at ease and pleased to be speaking? Does the way you look fit with the message of your speech? How can you look more comfortable? It may be as easy as dropping your shoulders or moving your head a little more when you speak. Do you need to gesture more, or less? Are there any annoying gestures you can eliminate, such as repeatedly pushing your glasses up or scratching your head?

Finally, look *and* listen. You'll see and hear how you can improve.

Practicing your delivery is hard work, but the rewards of preparation can't be overemphasized. One speaker I

If you're enthusiastic, your audience will be attentive, whether you're talking to a thousand people or to a handful.

coached said, "Thank goodness you made me do it again and again. When I finally stood up at the podium, I realized I knew more about my subject and my speech than anyone in the audience. In fact, I knew my speech cold. Even if I made a mistake, I felt so confident I knew I'd be able to cover it. Rehearsal made it possible for me to relax and enjoy myself."

If you can arrange it, stage one final dress rehearsal in the room where you will speak. It will allow you to become familiar with the layout of the room, the setup of the podium, the lights, the acoustics. If you can't arrange this final step, don't worry. You've worked hard. You're at ease with your speech. You're ready to go.

DELIVERING YOUR SPEECH

9

No matter how much or how well you've practiced delivering your speech, actually giving it will be different. Performance is not practice. Dress rehearsal can never be exactly the same as opening night. That difference, though, isn't necessarily frightening: it's the stuff exhilaration is made of.

Besides, there are techniques that will help you minimize the novelty of the situation, so that the energy you feel is something you can use, not something that stops you dead and silent in your tracks. Experience in speaking is one good way to get comfortable with these preperformance jitters. But there are other ways as well. Some are techniques directly related to speaking, while others focus on feeling good about yourself

CONSIDER WHAT YOU'LL WEAR

Dress appropriately for the situation—not too dressy, not too casual. Ask advice if you don't know what's right. Of course, in some instances, you won't have a choice. As valedictorian, you'll probably wear a cap and gown. At a black-tie dinner, you'll be formally dressed. But what about other occasions, such as a speech in class?

Wear something comfortable, something familiar, something you feel good in, rather than brand-new clothes. Remember you will want to be able to breathe freely, so loose is better than tight. Avoid close collars, ties that choke, and constricting necklaces. And remember that clanking jewelry will distract both you and your audience.

In general, dress up a little. It's an honor to be asked to speak, and while it might be corny to say that as you stand up in front of the group, it's fine to say "I'm honored to be here" by the way you're dressed.

Jackets add authority to both men and women. Wear yours over a neatly pressed shirt or blouse with a crisp collar; soft collars such as those on knit polo shirts rumple and look sloppy.

Grooming is as important as the clothes you wear. Hair that hangs in your eyes, glasses that constantly slip to the tip of your nose, dingy teeth, and dirty fingernails all say, "I don't care about myself—or my audience." And slipshod grooming can distract from what you're going to say.

Don't try a new hairstyle or get a drastic haircut the day before you speak—what if you hate it? It's probably best not to experiment too wildly with makeup, either. Do what you normally do, so you can feel at your ease. The more certain you are that you look good, the less you will have to think about it and the more energy you will have available to focus on your speech.

Now you're perfectly groomed and dressed. But you say you've been up the past three nights watching that late-night comic with the whacky skits? And over the weekend you skied nonstop, then crammed all night for a chemistry exam?

Exhausted is one of the worst things you can be when you have to give a speech. Rest both your body and your voice for at least a day before your performance. Better yet, think of your speech as an athletic event, and get in training—eating right, sleeping well—for at least three days ahead.

Be sensible about exercise before your appearance, too. It's okay to take a long walk, but don't start training for the marathon the day before you're on. You don't want to stand at the podium and have your muscles screaming at you.

Being tired takes its toll on your nerves as well as on your voice. Being rested will help keep your jitters to a minimum. It's hard to relax when you're tired; you feel as if you'll fall asleep if you let down for a moment. And not being able to relax makes nerves that much worse. Decide to be rested.

WHAT TO TAKE TO THE PODIUM

You'll have the text of your speech, of course. If you have typed it out, your sheets will be clipped together, not stapled, so you can slide one page behind the other as you read. If you're speaking from note cards, make sure they're numbered and securely fastened for your trip to the stage with a clip or rubber band.

You should also have a handkerchief with you, in case you sneeze or your eyes water or your palms or brow begin to sweat. Tissues tend to shred under this kind of pressure. A cotton or linen handkerchief is best.

Also consider taking along a piece of hard candy. Your mouth may get dry, your throat might feel itchy, or the muscles in your neck may get tight. Hard candy will help you avoid the coughing and throat clearing that tighten you up.

If you can arrange it, you might drink a cup of hot tea before speaking. And if a glass of water hasn't been provided for you at the podium, you might take one (carefully!) along.

Other props are certainly possible. It all depends on what you feel you need. One woman I know puts a pocket watch with a large clear face on the podium when she speaks, so she never runs over her time limit —or her audience's lunch break. Another carries a small jar of petroleum jelly, used to coat her dry lips and occasionally her front teeth. She says it keeps her lips from sticking to her teeth when her mouth gets dry. Still another speaker carries a smooth stone in his pocket, because it feels cool in his palm, helps keep his hands from sweating, and soothes his nerves.

You can take along whatever makes you feel more secure, though showing up at the podium with your teddy bear isn't encouraged. You don't want your audience to know you're *that* scared.

In fact, hiding your nerves is one of the best cures for them. Don't fidget as you wait for your turn to speak. You're onstage from the moment you enter the room, and you don't want the audience to catch you in a fit of panic. Sit with your feet on the floor, hands unclenched in your lap. Feel the chair supporting you, and breathe, deeply, slowly. If your palms are wet, by all means, wipe them with your handkerchief.

Talk yourself out of your nervousness. Most speakers give themselves mental pep talks while they're waiting to go on. Repeat one of positive things your practice listeners said, such as "You've got great enthusiasm," or "You have a lovely voice." Or tell yourself something that makes you feel more secure. "I know more about my subject than anyone else here. I'm the expert. I'm here to share my knowledge." You can tell yourself you look marvelous, you're smart, and you've worked hard. Make it positive. Make it short. And repeat it, silently, as much as you need.

When it's finally time to speak, rise, get hold of your

Don't forget to smile!

Use your hands and arms when you speak. If you are relaxed and confident, this often happens naturally.

speech, and walk serenely to the podium. No mugging or shuffling, please. Looking calm, after all, is half the battle. And self-possession breeds calm. Whatever jitters you feel, try to remember that they're natural. Everyone who gets up to speak feels, to a greater or lesser degree, exactly what you're feeling. It's a matter of learning to control it.

You've been nervous before and lived to tell the tale. And what, after all, is the worst that can happen? The audience is rooting for you, hoping you will be wonderful.

Stand calmly at the podium for a moment. Take a deep breath, perhaps a sip of water, then establish eye contact with the audience. Take them in.

After all your rehearsals, you should know the first few sentences of your speech by heart. Glance at your text, look out at the audience again, and begin. Remember to speak slowly and clearly. Remember to breathe.

If you're just normally nervous, that's usually all it takes. Once you're launched into your topic, your anxiety will fade and you can begin to enjoy the fruits of your preparation.

But what if you find yourself with a worse case of the jitters than you'd expected? Maybe a lot is riding on your performance or you didn't get enough sleep or the competition is fierce. Suddenly you find yourself more nervous than you expected to be. *Don't panic.*

Instead, get grounded. Nothing is more comforting in moments like these than the knowledge that your feet are still connected to the floor, and that the rest of you is connected to your feet. Breathe. It's your life force, your true energy source: use it. Buy time by taking a sip of water. If your palms and your forehead are covered with sweat, say "Excuse me," take a moment and mop yourself dry with that handkerchief. Remember that the audience cannot hear your heart pounding or see your knees shaking. Appear calm even if you can't be calm.

Consider that what you're feeling is not so much fear as a form of excitement. Enjoy the moment, if you can. Relish the edge of nerves; they will give you the power it takes to deliver a really dynamic speech. Hold onto the podium or a nearby table if you must. Establish eye contact with several members of your audience. Remember that they are human beings, not ogres, and that they have come to hear you speak. Don't dance around. Look as poised and confident as possible, glance at your speech, smile, and begin.

While you are speaking, remember to vary your intonation. Don't rush. Emphasize important points with your voice and with gestures. Move around a little; it will help you to relax.

Most importantly, look at your audience. Enjoy what you can of the experience. This is your moment. Shine.

AFTER YOU'VE FINISHED

Take a moment to acknowledge audience reaction. It will most likely be applause, perhaps wild, perhaps polite, but applause nevertheless. Take it in, and relish it. It is one of your rewards for a job well done. Smile at your audience and be seated.

Once you are offstage, don't fidget. Try to remain collected, calm, and poised. If you think you just gave the greatest speech ever, don't gloat. You earned the audience's approval. Acknowledge it, enjoy it, and sit down. No raising your arms over your head and clasping your hands triumphantly, please. You'll look more like a chimp than a champ.

If you are less than happy with your performance, don't take out your handkerchief and sob all the way back to your seat. You probably weren't that bad. And if you were, hysterics won't make things better. Maintain your dignity. You can always cry when you get home.

Better than berating yourself, however, learn from your experience. What went wrong? How could it have been prevented? What would make it easier, more fun, more interesting next time?

AND LATER

You'll feel a rush of energy after your speech is finished, a kind of high. It's partly relief that your performance is over. It's partly the pleasure of having been "on." It's the feeling that many performers live for. Enjoy it. You earned it.

Celebrate. Treat yourself to a book you've wanted, or a bubble bath, or new equipment for a sport or hobby. Indulge in a favorite food.

And, in a day or two, when all the excitement's behind you, take a few minutes to look forward. Imagine with pleasure the next time someone asks, "Say, would you be willing to give a speech?"

SUGGESTIONS FOR FURTHER READING

ON WRITING

Barzun, Jacques. *Simple & Direct: A Rhetoric for Writers.* New York: Harper & Row, 1975.

Brande, Dorothea. *Becoming a Writer.* Los Angeles: J.P. Tarcher, 1981.

Strunk, William, Jr., and White, E.B. *The Elements of Style.* 3d edition. New York: Macmillan, 1979.

Zinsser, William. *On Writing Well.* 3d edition. New York: Harper & Row, 1985.

SOURCES FOR QUOTATIONS

Bartlett, John. *Familiar Quotations.* Boston: Little, Brown, 1980.

Conlin, Joseph R. *The Morrow Book of Quotations in American History.* New York: William Morrow, 1984.

Fitzhenry, Robert I. *Barnes & Noble Book of Quotations.* New York: Barnes & Noble, 1981.

Kent, Robert W. *Money Talks—The 3,000 Greatest Quotes on Business from Aristotle to DeLorean.* New York: Facts on File, 1985.

Peter, Dr. Laurence J. *Peter's Quotations: Ideas for Our Time.* New York: Bantam Books, 1979.

Seldes, George. *The Great Thoughts.* New York: Ballantine Books, 1985.

SOURCES FOR FACTS

Asimov, Isaac. *Isaac Asimov's Book of Facts.* New York: Grosset & Dunlop, 1979.

Hatch, Jane, ed. *The American Book of Days.* New York: H.W. Wilson, 1978.

Lane, Hana U. *The World Almanac and Book of Facts.* New York: Newspaper Enterprise Association, 1984. Revised regularly.

U.S. Bureau of the Census. *Statistical Abstract of the United States.* Washington: United States Government Printing Office, annual.

ON VOICE CONTROL

Peacher, Georgina. *How to Improve Your Speaking Voice.* New York: Frederick Fell, 1966.

SAMPLES OF EFFECTIVE SPEECHES

Vital Speeches (magazine)
The Executive Speaker (newsletter—available from The Executive Speaker, P.O. Box 292437, Dayton, Ohio, 45429)

INDEX

ABOUT
THE AUTHOR

Margaret Ryan writes speeches for corporate executives and promotional material for their corporations. She also writes poetry and has won an award from the Poetry Society of America for the best sonnets written in 1985. She lives with her husband, Steven, and daughter, Emily, in New York City.